My Dear Janet,
You are the reason
this book is in your hands.

Without your encouragement,
it wouldn't be here. Thank
you for believing in me.

Love, Jerry

Accidental Travels of a Single Woman

by

Terry Woods

This book is dedicated to those who live in kindness and compassion.

Table of Contents

Introduction

Although always traveling for pleasure, I had another reason to travel after moving to Las Vegas. That's when I became allergic to the summer heat and my doctor gave me two options, "Take medicine or leave town."

If I took medicine and stayed home, it also meant spending a quarter of my life indoors without daily walks in the cool, fresh air. When it came down to it, leaving town every summer really became my only option.

After a few short trips and occasional visits with friends, I still had to find affordable places to stay for three months. Fortunately, luck was on my side when I discovered several European home exchanges and "The Affordable Travel Club" whose members live around the world.

Travel club hosts always welcomed me with an invitation to chat and enjoy tasty snacks with a refreshing drink or a glass of wine. Since hosts provide a B&B-like experience for a nominal fee, as a single person, I paid fifteen dollars per night, including breakfasts with my hosts.

Aside from email addresses and phone numbers, members were also asked to list their accommodations, hobbies, and interests in dining out with guests. A few travel hosts insisted on becoming my personal guides. They took me to their favorite spots and events where I had unusual adventures in the most unlikely places. Their kindness was the reason I came away with so many fond memories.

European home exchanges provided stays from a week to a month, or more. Although people usually swap homes at the same time, fate stepped in when an Italian man and two French couples requested non-simultaneous exchanges with me. During my month-long stays, I became part of their daily lives. Being embraced by such wonderful people was an enormous gift. Thanks to their generosity I had unusual and exciting experiences. They unfold as you begin reading this book.

Below the title of every chapter is the year in which each story was written. If you read the chapters in chronological order, the stories will flow easily with a clear understanding about people, places, and events.

Fate also had a hand in bringing my book into existence. When friends worried about me traveling alone in foreign countries, I wanted to put their minds at ease. Having kept a life-long diary, I just typed my foreign travel entries into a computer and sent them off as emails. Around that time, Janet and I met through our travel club. As an avid reader who devoured travel magazines, she asked if she could read my own travel adventures.

When Janet finished the last one, she spent the next nine years trying to convince me to publish them. So I really have Janet to thank for this book.

Although friends were concerned about my solo travels, they were still impressed by my courage to "go out there all alone." To me, courageous people are afraid; they just don't let their fear stop them from going for it anyway.

When I was a curious, naïve young woman, I dared myself to go out in the big wide world. I lived there in fear until the age of fifty. By then, I had three businesses under my belt and a lot of practice staying calm and using logic when necessary.

People asked me how I met such fascinating people in my travels. As life has taught all of us, everyone has a story to tell if someone is there to listen. Fortunately, people could feel my inborn empathy and concern for them. Since I was also a motivational speaker, perhaps my energy is what made it easier for us to connect.

Over the last sixteen years, my view of the world and life itself has certainly broadened. I am especially thankful for having explored the unknown where I found greater joy and a deep sense of inner peace.

Terrisima and the Blossom of Bellagio
2001

Without any hesitation whatsoever, I agreed to a one-month home exchange in Milan, Italy. Emilio was a retired language professor who offered a non-simultaneous exchange in May. He arranged to live with a friend while I stayed in his apartment. Since Emilio had extra room, he also suggested bringing a friend if I felt more comfortable.

After we signed off online, I called my dear friend Rhonda. Crossing my fingers, eyes and toes, I hoped she could join me.

Rhonda could hardly contain herself. "I don't believe this! Last month, in my positive thinking class, our teacher asked us to make a wish board. We put words and pictures on the board that expressed what we wished for. My biggest wish was for taking a trip to Europe!"

We laughed about how things worked in the universe. Both of us already knew we would be perfect traveling companions.

Rhonda attracted people like a magnet. Her blonde hair and large blue eyes drew them to her vivacious personality. If we needed directions, people went out of their way to help us. In several restaurants, Rhonda asked people sitting next to us if they could please decipher the menu. We usually joined them for dinner the next night in their favorite restaurants.

Emilio was always there for us. Twice a week, he took us to museums, monuments, churches and castles. Since Italy is the fashion capital of the world, he also took us to districts where stores were comparable to those on New York's Fifth Avenue. Although the designs were the newest in fashion, none were sold in America until three years after their first appearance in Italy.

Rhonda's son called a week after we arrived. Steven asked how she was doing.

"At home I feel invisible," she said, "but here, I feel like a young chickadee! Emilio has been so kind, taking us everywhere."

She turned to me with her son's reaction. "Steven said if we were ugly, he wouldn't show us a thing!" Rhonda and I laughed knowing that wasn't true.

"Italian people are full of life," Rhonda told her son. "And they don't hold in their feelings. It's such a joy to see people living life with such gusto."

Rhonda and I had a passion for dancing. She told Steven about the nightclub right across the street from Emilio's apartment.

"Last night we went to a dance club at midnight when things really got going. It was salsa night and the sexy men and women were dressed in the latest fashions. Professional dancers performed on stage and the whole place was in a dancing frenzy. We watched everything from the balcony where people could see everyone dancing below. Would you believe, we got home at three in the morning?"

She stopped talking when Steven asked her a question. "No," she replied smiling, "I never got pinched!"

The next morning, we took a train to Lake Como and a ferry to Bellagio, the most famous town on the lake. Stepping off the ferry, we decided to check into the hotel in front of us. Spending the afternoon walking through delightful shops, we resisted buying whatever we saw.

Our room in Hotel du Lac had a private balcony over-looking the lake. After dinner, we watched the flow of ferries, yachts and sailboats against the backdrop of the magnificent Italian Alps.

While relaxing in our chaise lounge, Rhonda began singing, "Oh, Solo Mio." Suddenly she stopped and looked up at me with tears in her eyes.

"Terrisima, I want to thank you so much for this amazing experience you have given me."

That was the first time Rhonda called me Terrisima, and she still does when we reminisce about Italy. In that euphoric moment, she also gave herself an Italian name, "The Blossom of Bellagio." It definitely fit.

After our return to Milan, we wanted to explore other cities. We decided to take a train to Paris for the day and then a train to Florence for two days.

Rhonda's heart was also set on visiting Austria. The day we were flying over the Austrian Alps toward Vienna, Rhonda looked at them from her window seat. Then, turning toward me, she began singing, "The hills are alive with the sound of music..." Her passion and exuberance rivaled Julie Andrews.

Two days later, we headed back to Milan and prepared for our trip to England. Emilio drove us to the airport when it was time to leave.

Holding back tears was difficult as I thanked Emilio for his extremely generous time. "Hopefully," I said, "I will come back, but only after you come to Las Vegas!" Both of us smiled in agreement.

Richard met us at the gate when Rhonda and I landed in London's Heathrow Airport. Since his parents were swapping homes with me simultaneously, they had made previous arrangements for Richard to fetch us at the airport and then drive us to their house.

After Richard left us to ourselves, Rhonda and I began looking through brochures on the kitchen table. His parents provided more than enough information about places to see and what to do during our stay.

We stopped in our tracks while looking through a brochure with pictures of Hartwell House, located an hour north of London. Built in the 1700's, eventually it became home to the aristocracy. King Louis XVIII had lived in Hartwell House from 1809 to 1814. It was turned into a hotel with a spa in 1989.

Rhonda and I looked at each other for half a second. Then we decided to splurge by spending one night in royal bliss.

As Rhonda continued looking through the brochures, she opened one with a list of antique shops. She reminded herself about finding an antique clock to grace her living room mantle.

The next morning, we wandered through three antique shops without success. In a smaller shop around the corner, Rhonda began talking with a handsome man who had appeared to be in his early fifties. She asked him if he knew where she could find mantle clocks. Phillip offered to help her find what she was looking for. He said he knew the area well since he had antiques for sale in several nearby shops.

By then, it was time for lunch. Phillip suggested eating together at an outdoor fish stand nearby where he referred to 'fish and chips' as 'fish and potatoes.' After we began eating, he told us the slang names of typical English words and phrases.

Phillip sat on a bench practically shoulder to shoulder with Rhonda as they ate with their fingers. I stood near Rhonda while enjoying my delicious fresh cod fish.

Chowing down his food, Phillip told me Rhonda was his china plate. He turned to her with a flirtatious look in his eyes.

Smiling modestly, Rhonda looked up at me, "Oh, I'm his china plate. I like that. Isn't that sweet?"

Looking at Rhonda playfully, Phillip explained, "That's slang for my mate."

When a car went by, he said, "There's a jam jar. That's slang for car." While they tasted each other's food and laughed together, Phillip sat even closer to Rhonda.

Since her divorce many years ago, Rhonda had barely been out in the world as a single woman. I believed her friendly personality was now being misinterpreted by Phillip.

At that point, he was also beginning to present a different picture of himself. His instant and intimate attention to Rhonda convinced me that he was a womanizer. After a few more hours, I imagined he might want to do business in the United States under the wing of an American woman. I recalled hearing stories about such situations.

By the end of the day, Phillip offered to take us to the greyhound dog races at the Wimbledon Stadium that night. Although we thanked him and declined, Rhonda accepted his offer to look for the clock of her dreams the following day.

Before Phillip came for her the next morning, I warned Rhonda about his potential hidden motives. "If he takes you to his house to see his antiques, please don't get out of the car. Just tell him how tired you are and that you need to go back to our place."

That's exactly what happened. I was relieved watching them pull into the driveway. Rhonda invited Phillip to come in the house and stay for a while. Feeling my distrustful energy directing him out the door, Phillip left within five minutes.

Fortunately, with his assistance, Rhonda had found the perfect mantle clock that day. So in the end, she was able to take her clock home along with a few flirtatious memories.

After a late lunch the next day, Rhonda and I were off to our adventure in Hartwell House. As the van pulled into the driveway, ninety-four acres of exquisitely landscaped grounds, ponds and pasturelands presented a picture right out of a storybook fairytale.

The cost of our suite was $450 for the night. It actually became a bargain when Rhonda commented about the photograph of our room. It didn't look like the one she saw in the brochure. The price was immediately reduced to $300.

The suite's 16-foot ceiling looked over our canopied, four-poster bed with cream-colored satin sheets. Filled with furniture and paintings from the 1700's, our entire room was paneled and graced with a large fireplace featuring a wood-carved hearth. The hallway was wide and long with a profusion of closet space on both sides. At the end of the hallway, a large, well-appointed bathroom featured metal towel bars to keep our towels warm.

In a heavy British accent, Rhonda asked, "Should I put on my evening gown now?" As usual, she was being playful.

"Oh, yes," I said with an equally heavy British accent. "We should have a spot of tea and crumpets by the fireside in the library, Dahling."

As we left our suite, Rhonda decided to walk down the stairs to the first floor. She waited for me to come out of the elevator before approaching each step slowly.

"I feel like I should be wearing a ball gown with a train," she said, fluffing up her imaginary gown as she stopped at each step briefly.

The grey marble steps were adorned with life-sized statues of seventeenth century royalty. With comedian Jack Benny in mind, Rhonda stopped mid-way and announced, "This is King Louis the eighteenth and I'm Rhonda the 39th!" Then, turning sideways, she pushed her imaginary train up in the air with a flick of her wrists.

Both of us felt free about having fun despite the extremely proper British atmosphere. When Rhonda reached the bottom of the stairs, she walked over to a baby grand piano in the hallway.

Leaning into the piano with her arm stretched across the top, Rhonda began singing. Just then, the hotel manager came by. We had seen him earlier in the library where King Louis XVIII sat and signed documents re-instating him as king of France.

The manager was dressed formally in a black tuxedo with a white shirt and black bow tie. Rhonda felt comfortable about taking his arm and said, "Look, Terrisima, here's our favorite person." He addressed me with a slight bow.

"Hello, I'd like to introduce myself. My name is Kevin. I'm Rhonda's butler. I do everything for her."

She was still holding his arm as Rhonda laughed and exclaimed, "I love it!"

Then, turning to me, she said, "Take a look at his tails!"

Kevin displayed them as he turned around and bowed deeply. Then he asked, "Are you enjoying your stay?"

When I nodded positively, he said, "I guess it takes a Scotsman to run an English hotel properly, eh?"

Since Kevin happily agreed to continue our joke about being Rhonda's butler, I decided to create a scene in front of the hotel's massive door. It was arched, deeply imbedded with metal cleats and the perfect backdrop for a video clip.

As my camera rolled, Kevin opened the heavy door with a friendly greeting. "Good afternoon and welcome to Hartwell House," he said, smiling into the camera.

Rhonda was standing behind Kevin. She peeked out and turned to him when he said, "Madam, your bath is running and dinner awaits you."

Kevin closed the door and then opened it for another 'take.' Facing my camera again, he explained, "I've been with Rhonda and the family for years."

Rhonda called out to me, "I'm never leaving!"

Turning to her, Kevin smiled and said, "I'll be up later to scrub your back." Then they laughed together as Kevin promptly closed the door.

Looking quite serious and opening it again, he gave me his farewell words. "We have to keep the riff raff out, you know," as he slammed the door shut.

After laughing together, it was finally time for Kevin to leave us. We thanked him profusely for making our day special and definitely unforgettable.

When Kevin left, Rhonda and I decided to look for more interesting rooms to explore. We found one with magnificent paintings, sculptures and plush furniture. By then, it actually felt like we were in a museum.

Rhonda picked up a beautifully framed photo and said, "Look, Terrisima. Here's the Queen Mum! She stayed here." It was our first glimpse of royalty who had been guests in Hartwell House over the years.

After exploring more rooms and admiring their magnificent décor from floor to ceiling, we returned to our suite for delicious late-night snacks provided by the hotel.

An hour later, two chamber maids knocked and asked to enter. We named them Frick and Frack. The thin, soft-spoken woman was Frick. She changed our towels. Frack was stout and outspoken. She closed the curtains and pulled down our sheets.

They let their hair down after Rhonda questioned them about our room. "President Clinton stayed in room sixteen," Frick said.

That left an opening for Rhonda. She asked boldly, "Was he with his wife or a girlfriend?"

Frack answered her question. "I believe his wife was here but we don't know if they stayed in the same room." Then she changed the subject.

"We also had the Emperor and Empress of China stay here. You are staying in room six," she said with an eerie laugh. "It's haunted, you know. People ask for this room because of that and its hidden walls."

Joining in, Frick said, "Sean Connery stayed in room fifteen."

Rhonda piped up about his movie, "I remember him in the movie, *"Goldfinger."* Didn't Shirley Bassey sing that hit song?" When Rhonda began singing a few bars, we cheered her on.

Then, Frick and Frack excused themselves politely and left.

It was getting late. "Time to call it a night in Hartwell House," Rhonda said wistfully.

I wasn't quite ready to sleep. After Rhonda got into bed, I went back into the library to enjoy the warmth of the fireside.

While watching the flames dance, a smile came across my face. When I thought about our stay, I imagined it was probably the first time Hartwell House ever saw the likes of two American women like us. I'd say they were pretty darn lucky.

Lookin' Back at Luckenbach
2001

Although no one warned us about getting lost in the woods, when Richard saw two buildings ahead, his wife Diane exclaimed, "We finally found Luckenbach!" It was a small hamlet located fifty miles north of San Antonio where they lived.

I was fortunate to be with two travel club members who were eager to show me Texas the way it was 'way back when.'

As Richard pulled off the dusty dirt road, one roughly-hewn wooden building came into view. It was set back and nestled among craggy oak trees.

As a crowing rooster strutted with territorial pride, I walked up to the front porch of a smaller building. Part of me felt right at home. The country setting was reminiscent of my Connecticut childhood on a dairy farm. Although I had spent most of my high school years in Brooklyn, New York, I still yearned for the sights, sounds, and smells of the country.

A tall, trim man stood in the doorway of the porch. His blue eyes stood out dramatically. They were set between his white cowboy hat and deep blue shirt. In jeans and cowboy boots, he looked exactly like a character out of the Old West.

His deep voice followed his wide grin as he said, "Welcome to Luckenbach, Y'all!"

Then he cleared the doorway for us to come in. Still smiling, he slipped behind the counter with an invitation. "Feel free to go out in the back room where we've got some great pickers and the coldest beer around this part of Texas." He was Virgil, The Store Guy. His business card called him that, too.

I asked Virgil how he came to be The Store Guy. He told me about his past candidly. As a younger man, he led the life of a real cowboy: bareback, saddle bronc and bull riding. After eight knee operations, Virgil had to give it all up. He started mining in New Mexico until he decided to deal cards in Bull City, Arizona. He wound up in the restaurant business a few years later.

Curious about the reason he came back to work in Luckenbach, I was touched with his answer about being a single dad. Virgil wanted to settle down and run his own ranch so he could put his son through college. He pulled out his wallet and flashed his son's high school picture. Then, looking up with the soft smile of a proud father, Virgil became wistful.

"Ya know the difference between being young and being old, don't ya, Ma'am?"

That was the first time a grown man ever called me Ma'am. I was told it was the way polite men addressed women in Texas.

"Well," he continued, "Young people are dreamin' and old people are rememberin'."

I asked him if he still did any riding. Without hesitation, he answered, "I sure have some great times riding my motor-sickles."

Virgil kept pretty busy. He told stories about Luckenbach's history, sold tourist items and acted as the security guard in the dance hall next door.

I learned a lot about Luckenbach from Virgil. Originally its population was three. In 1849, Luckenbach was taken over by the Engels, three German immigrants who turned it into a trading post for pioneer farmers and Comanche Indians.

In 1885, Luckenbach had a blacksmith shop and a school. A year later, the trading post was divided into three sections: the post office, a general store, and the beer joint.

14

I stood a few feet away from a white line which ran across the floor. It used to separate the post office from the general store. If people had beer in their hands, they had to stand behind the white line. Those first six feet sat on federal land and no one could drink on government property.

By 1904, Luckenbach's population increased to almost 500 people. It was practically a ghost town seventy years later when a group of Texans bought it for $30,000.

That's when Hondo Crouch, a beloved white-bearded character, proclaimed himself as the new mayor. He became a legend "in his own mind," as folks said around there.

Hondo told stories, sang songs and attracted thousands to his country western Camelot. His efforts to build a place for fun and music brought people from everywhere. His claim *"Everybody is Some Body in Luckenbach"* became a famous slogan.

After Texas country-rocker Jerry Jeff Walker came there in 1973, he brought fame to Luckenbach. He wrote a few songs in the back room and used the dance hall to record them. Other singers like Waylon Jennings followed suit. When he made famous the country western song of the same name, Luckenbach, Texas was finally on the map.

Willie Nelson celebrated Fourth of July holidays there with thousands of his friends. People packed the grounds to attend his authentic happenings: *The Valentine's Day Hug-Ins* and *The Ladies Chili Bust*.

Virgil asked us in his heavy southern accent, "Are ya' gonna be here for the daynce tonight?"

My ears perked up. I could hardly contain myself. My brain jumped for joy when my travel hosts went the extra mile by deciding to stay. The universe dropped a night of music and dancing at my feet and I was thrilled at the prospect.

Virgil's face lit up when he recognized someone coming through the door. He addressed the man with a hearty laugh. "If I was a dog, I'd be waggin' my tail."

Our time together was probably over. I figured it was best to head for the back room where a lot of pickin's were goin' on.

Before moving along, I looked at the souvenirs. Every sale item focused on Luckenbach slogans or country western singers who had been the town's Pied Pipers. There were postcards, t-shirts, and refrigerator magnets with slogans like, *"I Got Lost Trying to Find Luckenbach."* According to Virgil, they created the magnets after so many people said they couldn't find Luckenbach.

"Oh yeah, we sell a ton of them," he said. It was good to know that we weren't the only ones who got lost.

Then my hosts and I headed to the back room to experience Luckenbach in the present. Every inch of the A-framed space was covered with things that told stories about that tiny spot on earth. Two deer heads were mounted on one wall. Horizontal wood beams were layered with hundreds of baseball caps. A stuffed eagle hung over the middle of the room. It was positioned to look down on people below.

Each wall held old license plates, photos of country singers, and lighted beer signs. A huge "Lone Star Beer" sign had over two-hundred bullet holes in it. The sign, "Texas for Secession" was certainly a reminder of the past.

Five men were playing guitars at a table with empty beer bottles. They accompanied a young gal who played and sang the Patsy Cline oldie, *"I Fall to Pieces."*

Three men standing at the bar with beer bottles in hand were facing the music. One of them had a small, short-haired dog that was asleep by the stove in the middle of the room. When I noticed a red leash dangling between them, I wondered if the man might be more than he appeared to be.

When he began reciting cowboy poetry, he stood up and walked to the middle of the room. His Texas accent was very strong. Hard-pressed to understand the gist of what he was saying, I was a bit frustrated, wishing I could have grabbed more than a few words.

"I niver could kitch it," he concluded.

Frankly, it beat me about what I couldn't 'kitch,' but he was definitely quite entertaining. He reminded me of Will Rogers without the lasso.

The sun was going down as the back room filled up with people. I imagined most of them were there to hear the six-piece band in the dance hall at eight o'clock. I was getting excited just hearing the band warm up. Other people hung out at "The Feed Lot" where the smell of hamburgers, bratwurst and pulled pork filled the air.

The dance hall was built in 1882. It was still supported by its original massive wood beams. Lined with rows of fans and lights, they were the only modern fixtures in the place. Everything else was as old as the country hills.

Most of the building had been screened with large wooden shutters. They were lowered to keep the cool night air out at that time of year. During warmer weather, they were lifted and hooked into place to welcome the cool breezes and streaks of moonlight.

Tables and benches took up two-thirds of the dance hall space. That surprised me until I saw most of the people bringing food inside. After they sat down with their families, they were eager for some great country western music. Virgil stood in the doorway. He was ready to manage anything that came up.

Three couples took to the floor as the musicians started to play. The way it looked to me, most of the couples were basically just walking to the beat of the music. The country western two-step I had learned in Las Vegas was different from what I saw there.

Since learning the citified version, I figured it might benefit me to reconsider what those Texas hoofers were actually doing.

Twice in my life, poor dancers stepped on my toes so hard I wasn't able to dance for a month. That's not something a person forgets easily.

Although I was concerned about being stepped on in my open-toed sandals, I still hoped a man would ask me for a spin. Sitting impatiently, my hands and feet started tapping to the music.

When the second song began, The Store Guy was ready for me. Virgil was a gentle man aware of my needs. We danced without speaking as he led me around the floor effortlessly. His warm smile changed to a face of concentration as he guided and protected the lady in his care.

After two rounds with Virgil, a second man extended his hand to me. I took a deep breath and put mine in his. Adjusting easily to his dance style, we glided around the floor effortlessly.

"You're a top hand," he said.

I was curious. "What does that mean?"

Looking into my eyes, he explained, "It means someone is good in whatever they do and you're a very good dancer."

"Aw, shucks," I said with quiet cowgirl modesty. "That's because you're such a good leader." He didn't know how grateful I was for that.

The two cowboys made me feel comfortable. Taking me back to my seat, they were protective and aware of people nearby. After they sat me down and let go of my hand, they tipped their hats with a gracious, "Thank you, Ma'am."

They reminded me of my father, a man with great strength. He was a Connecticut dairy farmer who harvested 200 acres of alfalfa and corn, milked thirty cows twice a day, and helped birth their calves. My father was as gentle as he was powerful. He would always pet my head if I had been in pain or I needed to be soothed to sleep.

However, when I actually imagined my father dancing with me, I realized it wouldn't have been the same. He had two left feet.

Wearing my string sandals and black velour pants set me apart from other women on the dance floor. I wasn't a cowgirl, but no one seemed to care. As a matter of fact, someone was mighty happy about my being there.

It was a young man who danced alongside me with his partner. He wore a gray cowboy hat and a red bandana around his neck. There was a sparkle in his eye and a wide grin on his face. "Welcome to Texas," he said as he whirled on by.

That was my last dance. It was close to midnight. Diane said it was time for Cinderella to leave the ball. My early flight home the next day was a reality check.

As Richard drove away from Luckenbach, I sat back in my seat with gratitude for what he and Diane had done to make my trip unforgettable.

When I woke up the next morning, I realized leaving Texas wasn't going to be easy. As I sat on the plane before take-off, I thought about the last four days, wishing I didn't have to leave.

Texans had impressed me more than any other Americans. Other people felt the same way, especially those who worked for Southwest Airlines.

I found that out when a woman's voice announced our departure. She thanked everyone for their loyalty to Southwest Airlines which originated in Texas.

"Welcome aboard, all you great Texans. From flying to so many places, we know Texans are truly the friendliest people we've seen. We sure appreciate that. So by the end of this flight, all of us will have you spoiled rotten, just you wait and see."

By then, I was wiping tears from my eyes. It was a touching example of how to welcome and treat our fellow Americans.

When I was a child, I always heard that Texas and the word 'big' were synonymous. Texas was our biggest state, it had the biggest ranches, and men wore those big, ten-gallon hats. Now I knew it also measured the size of their hearts.

The Whole Truth
2002

My first contact with Uta and Joe began when they hosted our annual travel club dinner last year. It was held on the patio of their waterfront home in Gig Harbor, Washington.

When one of the club members said she and her husband were staying there for an entire month, my ears perked up. She offered to show me their sleeping quarters. To my amazement, the space was a large downstairs apartment with a wood-burning fireplace and a private patio overlooking Puget Sound!

After talking with Uta that day, I made arrangements for a month's stay the following summer. Living in my own waterfront apartment was a dream come true.

A week after my arrival, Uta told me about her life as a German baroness. She grew up in a castle on the Rhine River.

Her free-spirited nature didn't fit Uta's life as an aristocrat. She begrudged the stiff, artificial formality of it all. "I hated dancing the Minuet," she said with a hesitant smile.

She broke the aristocratic chain when Uta married Joe. Since he had been an Irish doctor, he was also unacceptable as a commoner, foreigner, and a man of a different faith.

Uta carried her stately elegance in a slender 5' 8" frame. It was topped with auburn hair gently coiffed in a page-boy cut. Every day Uta dressed as if she were going to an upscale luncheon. From morning til night, she wore casual woven hats and striking earth-tone jewelry. Her ensembles were complete with belted blouses, scarves, ankle-length skirts and slipper-style shoes. I watched her in disbelief as she cleaned and cooked without a splash or stain on her clothes.

My curiosity about Uta's heritage grew when I saw two large oil paintings in her home. In the hallway hung a Renaissance painting of a woman dressed in a jewel-studded taffeta gown. She was Uta's aunt, many times descended from the 1600's.

In the living room hung a larger than life painting of an older military man dressed in full uniform and brandishing a sword. Uta spoke proudly of her grandfather. Before 1916, he had been the Governor of Togoland in Africa.

I asked Uta about her father's military position in World War II. She said, "When my father was only 25 years old, Hitler assigned him to push the Russians from the German front to as far back as Moscow."

Uta became sad. "He rode on horseback during those severely cold winter months. The soil was too hard to dig trenches. My father had to kill his beloved horse, Izza, to provide meat for his starving men. When his soldiers died, he had to remove their shoes and take away their weapons."

Uta's story affected me emotionally. After composing myself, I felt compelled to ask her what her father knew about the unspeakable atrocities in the concentration camps.

Her voice became grave. "My father didn't know what was happening. Hitler kept his group small and close. He was written as swine in our history books, but no mention was made of what he did to those poor people in the camps."

I was surprised to hear what she was saying. She continued telling me about what had happened.

"When the war was over and my father found out about what happened there, he felt great shame and guilt. Everyone did. How could we ever rid ourselves of this? Many German people left our country when they could no longer live there with that shame."

Uta had been uncomfortable with the emotional stress of her past. "My father instilled such guilt in me that I was ashamed until I became nineteen years old. That's when I met Dr. Alan Ross, a Jewish physician. It was the day he told me, "Uta, let go of your guilt. It was the government's doing and it is history now. You must let go."

I asked Uta about life in Germany at the end of the war. "The French soldiers stripped my family of everything and our losses were never recovered," she explained.

"Fortunately friends helped us remove some of our family paintings and personal effects before they invaded us. Those things were eventually given back to us. When we were allowed to return to our castle, my father brought three-hundred people with us. They lost everything in the war and needed a place to live until they could rebuild their lives."

Good news came for Jewish people as well. The German government decided to help Holocaust victims and all their Jewish relatives. Since that day, thirty-five billion dollars has been given to hundreds of thousands of Jews who needed help to relocate, resettle and restore their lives.

My mind was in shock. *Why didn't I know this? I never read about that and no one ever told me those facts.*

Joe said most people probably didn't know this information. But he said I could find it on the internet if I knew what to search for. That's exactly what I did. Joe was right.

I had always received emails from well-meaning Jewish friends who warned me to "never forget" what happened. But I didn't know the German people adopted the same motto. Their shame was so great they didn't want any German citizen to forget the atrocities that had been committed.

After becoming aware of these truths, I felt free from my past. I thought about what Uta shared with me and was grateful for her trust and honesty in helping me get there.

I also learned an important lesson. When I want to dig for the whole truth, it may not be easy if the hole is deep.

Grazelda Penelope Stein
2002

An impish smile came across Ernie's face when I told him about my new GPS. He thought it would be fun if I gave it a name.

Seconds later, he blurted out, "I know what you could call her. Grazelda Penelope Stein!"

His wife, Lil, agreed as I gave it some thought. Come to think of it, they were right. That really was a great name for the female voice emanating from my new technological marvel.

Except for my childhood dolls, I never talked to inanimate objects or gave them names. I must admit, however, to being amused by people who grab their dashboards in full body embraces while thanking them because their cars didn't break down that day.

After telling another friend about my newly named GPS, she preferred to call her GyPSy. Thinking of me as a traveling gypsy, she figured the GPS lady and I were kindred spirits.

Then another friend listened to the GPS voice and said it sounded harsh. She started turning the knobs for different options and finally chose a British man's voice. Later that day, I opted for the female British voice. Frankly, I was definitely not ready to listen to a man tell me where to get off.

What was the best part of my new stress-free life? No more struggles trying to read a map! There weren't any flat places to lay out a map easily in a car. Trying to fold it up again was the worst part. Each map started out looking like the size of an envelope. After finding the directions and trying to fold it up again, the map was the size of a briefcase. Totally frustrated and abandoning all hopes of retracing the folding patterns, I just shoved the crumpled mess under the seat.

Although Map Quest had been a life-saver for years, I still wrote the directions in large print on a sheet of paper and placed it on the passenger seat. The directions had to be visible from the steering wheel as well as safe from falling under the seat or flying right out the window.

Unfortunately, I also had a poor sense of direction. Since I never grasped the idea of north, south, east and west, I suffered with great frustration. If a person said, "You will see a supermarket on the southeast corner," I simply said thanks and drove away in total ignorance.

Thanks to Grazelda, I didn't have to ask for directions any more. Gone were the days of grabbing the attention of people in other cars or stalking them on the street. I no longer had to find gas stations where half the people didn't know where anything was anyway. Although I had a 50-50 chance of meeting someone who knew the directions, it was still worth it. Anything was better than fighting with maps.

I was always grateful and relieved when people gave me detailed directions, especially when they knew the name of the following street. I waited patiently for their last bit of information. "If you miss the turn, the next street will be..."

I was stumped the first time I heard Grazelda's gentle voice say, "Recalculating." I quickly realized she was telling me where to turn to get me back on course. There was no criticism, no judgment and no one telling me how I messed up. There were no caustic remarks like, "You jerk, how could you miss that turn?" No, none of that stuff. It was simply a nice voice helping me find my way.

Needing a ladies room, I turned off the highway at the next rest area. Before getting out of the car, I apologized to Grazelda, wishing I could explain my reasons for not following her exact directions at that point.

Then, hearing her say, "Recalculating," actually made me talk to her out loud.

"Wait a minute! After I find a bathroom, I'll be right back!" Filled with guilt knowing Grazelda didn't understand me, I still waited for her to get upset and yell, "Hey, make up your mind!"

A year later, I visited Lil and Ernie again. They lived in the small town of Jacksonville in southern Oregon. Despite its population of 3,000, Jacksonville is known for its history of the old West and the Britt Festival concerts under the stars. Years ago, I lived in nearby Ashland where I published a monthly news magazine. Since I only lived 30 minutes away, my visits with them were frequent.

While turning onto Jacksonville's main street, I informed Grazelda that I could take it from there. It wasn't necessary to remember the name of the street where I turned left to get to their house. I just had to look for the landmark on that corner. It was a neon sign with the words "Jacksonville Tavern."

While approaching the corner, I saw a different tavern sign there. I kept driving, assuming a senior moment had just come over me.

Driving further, I saw the Jacksonville Tavern sign, but it was in the middle of the block! Now positive that I actually did have a senior moment, I turned left at the next corner.

Grazelda was recalculating and insisted I turn left again at the next street corner. That didn't make sense. It was the first time my doubts about Grazelda's directions took over. I ignored her while remembering what people told me about a GPS. It wasn't correct all the time.

After passing the next street, Grazelda recalculated again. She blabbered on about turning left at the next opportunity. Since this

Grazelda Penelope Stein

was her first mistake, I was willing to let it go. After all, no one is perfect.

Grazelda kept insisting I turn left at the next street. After my second refusal, I finally put it all together. The Jacksonville Tavern had been moved to the middle of the block and a different tavern opened on the corner where I usually turned left.

Wishing I hadn't tuned out Grazelda's directions, my apologies were profuse, "I'm so sorry I ever doubted you!" After turning left at the next street, a pact was in order.

"I promise to listen to you from now on, Grazelda," I said in a serious voice.

Three days later, I drove to Ashland to stay with other friends. Needing cash from a bank branch closest to their home, I located one in the Yellow Pages and asked Grazelda for directions. While turning at the corner onto the designated street, it became obvious that I was in a residential area.

As Grazelda announced my arrival, I concluded that she didn't give me the correct address. Chalking that one up as her first mistake, I reminded myself that a GPS was not always reliable.

After settling in for the day, out of curiosity, I checked the Yellow Pages. When I realized the error was mine, my guilt returned knowing I had put the wrong address into Grazelda's brain. *How could I have accused her of being wrong again when she had yet to fail me?*

For the first time, I realized something important. Grazelda never steered me wrong. She always spoke with kindness in her voice and accepted my human imperfections. Come to think of it, she understood me better than anyone. I think I'm in love.

28

Italian Road Sign Magic
2002

This year, although Emilio's schedule prevented him from coming to Las Vegas, he invited me to stay in his Milan apartment for another month. He was just as gracious in his efforts to fill my days with interesting places to explore while teaching me about Italy's history.

One day, Emilio suggested visiting a monastery in Certosa. The abbey was located in the province of Pavia, not far from Milan. Although Certosa was less than an hour away, it took Emilio two hours to find it.

Jokingly, he claimed to have had early Alzheimer's. Actually, Emilio just had a problem getting lost. On city roads, it didn't happen as often.

I'm not saying Emilio could get lost in a paper bag, but he pushed the envelope by asking the right question of the wrong people. Rather than ask those in cars, he stopped people on foot or bicycles. Many of them probably didn't own a car.

When Emilio stopped friendly people along country roads, they responded loudly, waving their hands with wild gusto in typical Italian gestures. Such sweet smiles and genuine concern they had for our good fare. As we drove away, I commented on how concerned they were by taking the time to direct us while standing in the hot sun.

"Yes," he agreed, "but they also knew **nothing!**"

Laughing out loud, I realized how easily I was fooled by their earnest display of theatrical confidence.

Actually, being fooled was the major reason we got lost. Many Italian road signs, especially in rural areas, were actually designed to fool you into believing something was there when it really wasn't. Road signs were a true case of, "Now you see them, now you don't."

Most signs enticed drivers to their first posting. People continued with absolute confidence, believing the signs would be there as they came around crucial corners. Actually, quite often there were three roads ahead without any signs about which of the roads to take.

We spent those two hours being fooled again and again. At some point, we actually looked forward to seeing how well we would be fooled while approaching the next intersection.

It was hard to say which magic trick was better devised. Were the signs fooling us into believing they were really and truly telling us where to go?

A sign seemed to point to the left… or was it to the right? First it said Pavia was this way, but then it never mentioned Pavia again. We came around the corner with a choice of two more roads without signs. Perhaps we were better off without any at all.

By the time laughing hysteria set in, we had the funniest moment of all. It was an invitation to a circular turn which led to signs directing us to the left…or was that to the right?

It left us cross-eyed trying to see which way the arrow was actually pointing. Once again, I realized we had become an easy target, as if an imaginary voice said, "Gotcha!"

Actually, there was only one sign to Certosa. It had also been magically misplaced. It was facing in the wrong direction when people were coming from Milan. They could only see that sign if they had driven into Pavia, made the U-turn, and started to head back toward Milan.

Just before Emilio made the turn, he was completely frustrated and considered heading back to Milan. After he made the turn and saw the sign to Certosa, he scratched his head in disbelief.

At that point, he also felt relieved when he understood what had happened. Suddenly the last two hours searching for Certosa became meaningless as Emilio forged ahead to the abbey.

I certainly enjoyed visiting the monastery, but something else left an impression on me. After remembering how often we were fooled by road signs, I came away with one thought. *Those Italian road sign magicians deserve a huge Christmas bonus!*

The Other Side of Paris
2003

Thanks to another home exchange, I spent one month with a delightful French family. They lived in a Paris suburb bordered by the Versailles forest. Their stunning home looked more like a French chalet. My favorite place was spending time on their sprawling back porch. From there, I enjoyed watching all of the goings-on around the large public pond below.

Anne and her husband Jacques, an orthopedic surgeon, couldn't do enough for me. They insisted I have every meal with them, join in family celebrations, and go on week-end outings to experience Paris fully. Yvonne, their cook and housekeeper, fussed over me as if I were American royalty.

Jacques couldn't understand why I felt content at home when Paris had so much to offer. Anne spent a lot of time in Paris. As an extrovert, she favored the city life.

When I spent time in Paris, I was usually part of a crowd where many people weren't French. Most often, they were tourists sitting in cafes while watching other tourists who were walking by. In turn, those who walked by the cafés were looking in at the tourists sitting inside.

It didn't make sense to Jacques and Anne that I enjoyed strolling around their lush gardens and taking walks around the pond where French life surrounded me.

At one end of the pond, a charming restaurant and small cafe were open for lunch and dinner. There were always people riding bicycles, scooters and horses. Others jogged, fished or had a picnic while feeding the ducks.

By staying closer to home, I met interesting people like Zoe. We met while walking around the pond in opposite directions. The second time around the pond, she stopped and complimented my hair. That was the beginning of our friendship. Zoe pointed to her house at the end of the block and invited me to see her recent paintings. We spent the next three hours talking about our love for art.

The following week, she took me to a small museum nearby. It was the original home of French painter Gustav Moreau whose works were permanently displayed there. When I told her about my visit to the Louvre, Zoe understood why our visit to Moreau's museum was a welcome relief for me.

The Louvre is the world's largest and most congested art museum. The entrance fee of $7.50 provides a day's stroll through what should take a week. For me, spending two hours there was all my brain and eyes could absorb.

Some people walked past pieces of art with barely a glance. They weren't interested in looking at them or understanding what the artists were trying to convey. Their major focus was in photographing them despite signs asking them to refrain from taking photographs.

Many people walked quickly past paintings, as if hurrying through each room to make sure they saw everything. Maybe they wanted to feel like they got their money's worth. Or perhaps they wanted to tell folks back home they went to the Louvre. Frankly, they could have saved a lot of time if they went directly to the bathroom and left. Then they could have told everyone they went to the Louvre and they wouldn't be lying.

Typically, when visitors first arrived in the Louvre, they waited on line for at least an hour to get past security. Then they waited to take the escalator into the lobby, followed by waiting in line to buy a ticket. The next segment included waiting their turn to take an escalator to the first area of what they thought was an all-day tour.

Visiting the Louvre was definitely a huge undertaking. There were sardine-packed crowds, seemingly endless stairs and a cascade of escalators. Visitors were given a flurry of maps to educate them about where everything was located on two levels in each of their three huge buildings.

Most tourist offices suggested traveling to the Louvre by bus or the subway. Unfortunately, all they would see were dark tunnels or scenery passing by quickly.

My preference was the two-mile walk from the major tourist office near the Arc de Triomphe. The walk included major Paris landmarks: the Champs Elysees, La Place de Concorde, and the Tuileries Gardens. Everything had been built in a straight line so people didn't need a map and they couldn't get lost.

Famous fountains, monuments and government buildings lined the walkways with several shops and cafes. In the smaller parks, children floated boats in ponds while adults sat on benches feeding the ducks. When I arrived at the Louvre, it was three-o'clock. The crowds had dwindled along with the entrance fee of only $5.00.

Like food, both French and Italian people believe life should be savored slowly. After experiencing their cultures close-up, I whole-heartedly agreed. That's why their meals were usually two hours long. Sometimes, I wonder if we Americans ate what was on our plates slowly, perhaps our lives might be different as well.

Consider the fact that the French and Italians also receive five-week paid vacations every year. When a child is born, couples receive paid leaves for one year. If people are fired from a job, the government provides half their salary for thirty months while they seek other employment.

It's much easier for French people to enjoy life with those government provisions. Their pace is also slower and less stressful. That's why their famous phrase "Joi de Vivre" is popular. It means "Joy of Life." That's what they live by and the reason I love Paris.

Music and Castles in the Air
2003

Zoe invited me to a private concert given by her friend, Jean-Efflam Bavouzet, the world-famous French concert pianist. Every year, he performed for mutual friends at a castle in the beautiful Normandy countryside.

Thirty years ago, when Zoe aspired to be an actress, her theater buddies bought the four-hundred year old castle to use as a performance center. After their dream faded, Pierre and Jacqueline kept the castle and turned the upper floors into their family residence. They still used the bottom floor for dinner parties and concert performances in the castle's two largest circular halls.

On that Sunday, Zoe arrived with her home-made salmon quiche in hand and two sons in tow. Pierre and Jacqueline, now philosophy teachers, sat outside with two other friends enjoying cognac and relaxing in the sun.

Ten acres were sitting behind them as one rectangular field. The entire space was bordered with trees. In the far right corner, a stable housed four horses.

Although a stranger there, I was welcomed with greetings bestowed upon anyone accompanied by a French friend. After introductions were made, a line of children suddenly appeared and came toward us.

They were directed by their parents to present themselves to me. Before I could turn around, there they were, lined up behind each other. Six young girls presented me with sweet smiles and kisses, twice on each cheek.

A few minutes later, the girls walked away slowly. Then, while holding hands, they pranced over the newly cut grass. Zoe's boys followed behind until they saw a huge tree with wide-spread branches touching the ground. It was perfect for climbing.

The children were called for lunch twenty minutes later. They cheerfully helped set the table. Then two women brought out an array of quiches, bib lettuce and French bread with wine. One woman came over with a basket filled to the brim with dessert: dark sweet cherries from a nearby tree.

During our lunch, I told Zoe about my joy in listening to the recorded music coming from an open window inside the castle.

"It's not a recording," she said. "You're listening to Jean-Efflam. He's practicing for his performance later."

That's when I got up and excused myself politely. "Excuse moi, si vous plait," I said softly as I turned to leave.

At that point, I was eager to continue listening to Jean-Efflam's music. It was also a relief from the fast-paced French conversation between Zoe and her friends.

After walking over to the open window where Jean-Efflam was playing, I sat down on the grass. Then I decided to stretch out right under the window sill. Closing my eyes and becoming blissfully relaxed, I listened to him play beautifully.

When he took a break, he walked over to the window and gazed out at the scenery. Then Jean-Efflam returned to his practice session for another half-hour.

By five o'clock, fifty other friends had arrived. Everyone brought home-made casseroles and desserts for dinner which was scheduled to follow the concert.

Zoe pulled me aside to show me the upper levels in the castle. We climbed the old marble steps toward the first upper level. Several original doorways were still intact. Zoe explained that others had been replaced 200 years ago. Circular towers, untouched over the years, were used as storage areas. Wooden inlaid floors had been replaced with modern tiles. Others creaked under foot as their pieces threatened to give way.

When it was time to go downstairs, Zoe was excited with anticipation. Wearing a huge smile, she told me, "It's time for the concert to begin!"

Everyone took a seat in a large circular room at the other end of the castle. Each chair faced a beautiful Steinway piano.

Since the chairs were hard with wooden backs and unpadded seats, I decided to sit in the rear of the room. If I needed a break during the one-hour performance, I could get up easily without disturbing anyone. When I saw an empty couch along the far wall, it beckoned me.

After laying my body down comfortably, the concert began. That's when I closed my eyes and listened to Beethoven played more magnificently than I could ever remember.

When the concert was over, everyone moved into another large room where dinner had been arranged along several tables. If I'd known earlier that dinner would be an irresistible mouth-watering feast, I would have eaten less bread during lunch!

My eyes were enticed by an array of foods I'd never seen before. There was a Georgian dish of red beans with cilantro, a pineapple and artichoke dish with Indian spices, and an eggplant concoction in a rich sauce of pureed vegetables, just to name a few.

It was hard to believe the desserts hadn't been purchased from a fine French bakery. A pear strudel, an apple tart, and a chocolate mousse with large chocolate chunks sat on the first table. A strawberry custard pie and a raspberry cream pie were next in line. The last table displayed a cherries jubilee cake and a six-inch chocolate cream-cheese mousse cake that looked like it would melt in my mouth. By then, it was obvious that I would consume at least one small piece of each dessert.

Before dinner started, I wanted to tell Jean-Efflam how much his concert pleased me. Everyone knew him well, so there were no lines of hand-shaking congratulations. I was relieved hearing how well he spoke English and approached him when the last person finished their conversation.

Before I had a chance to say anything, Jean-Efflam asked, "Weren't you the person lying down?"

Stunned into silence, I thought about what to say next and wondered how he knew that I was lying down on the couch during his concert.

Questions began rushing through my brain. *How could he see me back there? Did he think I was sleeping out of boredom?*

He saw my bewildered look and said, "On the grass, outside the window this afternoon."

My brain spent a few seconds in shock. *Of course! So that's what he meant! How silly of me!*

I answered him quickly, "Oh, yes, you're right. I was."

He laughed. "You were spying on me, eh?"

Although he was teasing me, I wanted him to know about my respect for his privacy. "I didn't even peek in the window. I was careful not to disturb you or appear to be nosey."

As we shook hands, his smile was warm and sweet.

Then someone came up to him and drew his attention away. I took that as a perfect cue to leave graciously and have dinner.

After filling my plate with samples of each dish, I sat down at an empty table. Within minutes, all the remaining seats were taken.

Some men were dressed casually with ascots while others wore suits. The conservative guests loosened up after dinner and several glasses of wine. An English-speaking woman sitting next to me said the entire table was filled with life-long friends.

She was a journalist for an international television company. Her husband, a music composer, sat directly across the table from us. His friends sat to his right and left. One was a cinematographer.

His wife was an English professor who taught at the university. Another friend taught eighteenth century medicine. He sat near his wife. She was an anthropologist who conducted research on modern pain relief in French hospitals.

There I sat, surrounded by a table of intellectuals. Frankly, they were simply a bunch of really nice people. They were probably like those people who enjoyed a similar life hundreds of years ago.

I imagined the scene was pretty much the same when most of the men had high collars and the women wore formal dresses. They must have been pretty uncomfortable on a day like that when the temperature kept rising.

To me, it was a perfect example of how people are just people, then and now. Surely all of us are alike when we sweat on a hot summer afternoon.

The Art of Viewing Art
2003

Zoe asked, "Would you like to go to the Giverny countryside to see where Claude Monet made his lily pad paintings?" It was a rhetorical question. Zoe knew he was my favorite impressionist painter. She wanted to show me where he had lived and worked.

My first glimpse of Monet's flower gardens took my breath away. As an avid gardener, I was in awe of what had been created there. It was apparent that each variety of flowers was selected for its color, height, depth and when it blossomed. While enjoying the magic of the flower gardens, my eyes followed their long lines up to Monet's house. On our way to his famous Japanese bridge, we passed a huge vegetable garden soaking up the sun.

When we walked onto the bridge, I saw white and pink lily pads floating on top of the pond below. Other varieties had been imported to create the effect Monet wanted in the foreground of the arched bridge. He kept the waterlilies pruned so they wouldn't grow into each other. They became his favorite motif to paint.

Looking further out from the bridge, I knew where Monet positioned himself as he painted. He simply sat in his rowboat along the edge of the pond. Standing in the middle of the bridge, I felt transferred to another place in time while imagining Monet in his boat, sitting across the pond from me.

Zoe suggested moving on to visiting his house. As we entered, I was surprised there were none of Monet's paintings hanging on the walls. Throughout his home, Asian sketches hung in almost every room. It was Monet's favorite art. Although he never visited Japan, he was inspired by its beauty and had assistance in choosing Japanese plants for his pond.

The decision to live in Giverny was made by his second wife. She hoped living in the countryside and being surrounded by beautiful gardens would lift Monet's spirits while he grieved the loss of his first wife. Fortunately, his second wife also provided the path for his famous lily pad paintings.

Zoe and I headed back to Paris after enjoying lunch in a charming restaurant outside Giverny. She was eager to show me Monet's paintings in the D'Orsay Museum.

My senses were heightened when I saw the first Monet painting. My nose was close enough to touch his rich, green lily pad paintings. As I leaned over the railing ever so slowly, I tried not to tempt the alarm system.

Standing a few inches away from his canvas, I saw a fraction of what Monet saw. Most of us would see gentle waves of blue and green. What Monet saw close up was not what we could see from there. We had to stand back ten feet to see that his painting looked like a photograph.

Most paintings from the 1400's through the 1600's were much like Rembrandt's works which also looked like photographs at a distance. However, they also looked like photographs whenever someone stood close to them. To me, that's what made Claude Monet a genius. Until that day, I also didn't know he was one of the few painters who earned a living from his work.

Stepping around the corner to view my first Van Gogh painting, I was drawn in by his three-dimensional thick dashes of paint in vibrant colors. I realized how stilted and one-dimensional his paintings were in magazines and re-prints. His use of bold, black outlines to create his striking, eerie style helped me understand why he was rejected during his life time.

At that point, I also realized why some painters became famous while others remained obscure. Aside from obvious talent, the reason for their success was basically a matter of promotion. Certainly there were painters as talented as Van Gogh and his colleagues; but they didn't live in Europe and didn't have the luck of good marketing.

By nature, artists aren't generally good salespeople anyway. They need someone who will get out there and make it happen. While wandering through galleries and seeing famous paintings, I just assumed those artists had really good agents.

Portrait of an Artist
2003

French artist Michelle Auboiron is known for her work as a contemporary painter. Depending on the size of her paintings, their values range from $3,000 to $20,000. When Michelle travels to a chosen destination for her next project, she creates one painting a day and forty paintings in fifty days. She selects only natural and man-made structures as her subject matter.

When Michelle created a huge canvas of the outdoor Las Vegas Neon Boneyard, I was there. She was excited about making a painting of the hotel landmarks from her favorite 50's era.

Michelle's way of painting was interesting to watch. First she stood with her back to the subject. As she turned to look at each scene, she memorized what she saw. Then, turning to face the canvas, Michelle painted what was in her memory. Her painting was complete in five hours without a break of any kind.

We met through Michelle's request for a non-simultaneous home exchange. She wanted to stay in a convenient home for one month during her art exhibit in Las Vegas. Although she spoke little English, whatever she wanted to say was interpreted by Charles, her partner of twelve years.

Charles complemented her both in love and work. Michelle painted and Charles photographed her while she painted. They toured the world together. Her website is awesome thanks to her Charles who was also its graphic designer.

When Michelle had been commissioned to make the Neon Boneyard painting in Las Vegas, she also agreed to bring ten of her paintings for exhibit in The Charleston Heights Art Center and The Marjorie Barrick Museum.

It would have been too expensive to ship her paintings. So she and Charles removed them from their frames, rolled them up individually, and carried them onto the plane in separate tubes. After arriving in Las Vegas, they stretched the paintings and put them back onto their frames in my garage. Two days later, they were on exhibit.

She and Charles fell in love with Las Vegas years ago when Michelle made ten paintings of the 50's motels on Freemont Street. Several are displayed on her website.

Michelle's style of painting gave me the incentive to draw attention to her work. I used to imagine what it would be like to be an artist's agent. After sharing my curiosity with Charles, I spent the next two weeks calling art galleries in other cities.

Charles told me it wasn't easy to get bookings, especially since Michelle's paintings were very large and required a lot of wall space in a gallery. I also found out it could take two years before paintings were actually exhibited.

Over the next few weeks, I called a local newspaper. The reporter interviewed Michelle at The Charleston Heights Art Center. The story was printed two days later.

Then I contacted a local television station. Their camera crew came to The Charleston Heights Art Center for an interview with Michelle, which appeared on the local news that night.

Many years ago, Michelle made a beautiful painting of the El Cortez Hotel in downtown Las Vegas. While she and Charles were still in town, I called the hotel owner and arranged a dinner meeting for all of us. I crossed my fingers hoping he'd purchase the painting and hang it next to the registration desk.

After deliberating for several days, he decided not to buy it. During that process, I learned a lot about what went on in the art world.

At times, it could be a difficult, time-consuming and expensive process. My small taste of it satisfied whatever curiosity I had about being an artist's agent. So I removed my head from the clouds and made my way back to earth.

During their final week in the United States, Michelle and Charles traveled to California and Arizona. They wanted to look at potential subjects for future paintings on a follow-up trip.

After returning to Las Vegas, once again, they prepared the remaining paintings for safe travels home. When Charles brought the last painting into the house, he said Michelle wanted to give it to me. It was one of the Grand Canyon series she had painted on a previous trip to Arizona.

I tried to refuse several times knowing the painting was valued at $4,000. Charles insisted and said it would make Michelle happy if I accepted her gift.

The striking, powerful painting of light and dark earth-tones had been a favorite of mine on Michelle's website. Now it hangs on a large wall in my dining room. Whenever I admire it, I stand in awe of Michelle's talent and her extreme generosity.

Sleepless Singles
2003

In my late fifties, I decided to take a ten-day Caribbean cruise with a program designed for single people. Those willing to have a roommate were given a 50% discount by sharing half the cost of the cabin.

Being a light sleeper, I agreed to share a cabin if the woman didn't snore. The booking agent assigned a cabin mate and suggested making contact to get to know each other.

A few days later, I called Cathy. She was a bubbly, 56-year-old British gal with a great sense of humor. I was elated about sharing a cabin with her.

In case she snored, I offered to turn the television up to drown her out. Agreeing to that arrangement, Cathy added, "Actually, I don't snore unless I haven't had enough rest. But don't you worry now. Nothing is more important than having fun."

The cruise hosts provided our group with pre-planned activities. Playful games were set up to pit the sexes against each other which were then followed by question and answer sessions to draw them closer together. During the evenings, there were karaoke nights, themed dances, and cocktail parties with complimentary drinks.

Many singles took the cruise for shipboard romances. Several women made themselves enticing targets. They strutted around the dance floor in low-cut, short dresses. Others wrapped themselves around poles like Las Vegas strippers.

One afternoon at the pool, an announcement about a dance contest caught my attention. Six male volunteers paraded themselves down a short flight of circular stairs. They wiggled their way toward six female volunteers waiting on the deck. While dancing in their bathing suits, the men smiled at women who rubbed their chests and shoulders as they moved down the line.

Their simulated bumping and grinding session had no resemblance to dancing. Filmed by a cruise host, their sexual moves could be seen for five days on television sets in every cabin.

The most aggressive men on the ship attempted to partner with disinterested women like myself. A few kissed my hand while telling me how hot I looked. They found their way to my dinner table where I politely turned them away.

As if rotating through a revolving door, they moved on to other prospects without any hesitation. Eventually, those men realized most women were not willing to spend the night in their cabin. Cathy had a great attitude. She flirted with men casually and took none of them seriously.

Things went well for the two of us until we had problems in our cabin. Cathy didn't snore, but a rattling noise kept both of us awake. The sound seemed to be a vibration against the metal trim along the ceiling while we were at sea.

Although intermittent, the noise left me sleepless and walking around like a zombie. The next day, I fell asleep on a bus tour and then on the grass during a lecture at a Jamaican coffee plantation.

After six days, the noise caused severe sleep deprivation. At that point, one might wonder how that situation could have continued for so long without a solution.

Actually, the noise stopped temporarily, just before someone came to fix it. It reminded me of the broken television set that worked fine after the repair man arrived.

Unfortunately, the only repair man authorized to fix the problem couldn't hear the noise. Other men who were sent to locate the noise actually heard it, but they had no authority to fix it.

That's when an Italian tech crew climbed into the rafters to find the rattle. They heard the noise, but they couldn't stop it.

The next day, we received a long letter of apology for our inconvenience. It included the assurance that all cabins were sold out which meant we could forget about changing cabins.

The letter ended with, "If we can be of help, please do call." After dinner, I decided to speak with the head honcho, the decision-maker, the person who needed to move mountains for us.

An hour later, he returned my call. Although insisting the metal ceiling trim be removed hoping the vibration might stop, I executed my back-up plan.

"Please don't say every cabin is sold out. Cruise lines usually leave two cabins available in case of an emergency," I explained.

He answered with typical corporate mentality, as if he were addressing a totally unaware woman. "We don't do that. This is a business."

My mind was taken aback with his comment. *What did he mean by that? Was he trying to confuse me?*

I picked up where he left off. "You could solve that problem if your business charged an extra dollar per passenger to cover the cost of keeping two cabins empty on each sailing."

He agreed, changed the subject, and offered to reduce our bill by $100.

I tried to stay calm. "After days without sleep and hassles about getting the right person to eliminate the noise, is this all you are willing to do?"

He had no immediate answer. "Well," he finally responded, "this is only an initial offer. Let's see what my technicians report after the trim is removed. Then I will get back to you."

Although he continued to insist there were no empty cabins, nevertheless, he now offered to look further.

"Perhaps there are some group bookings in which people didn't take the cruise," he explained further.

Minutes later, he called to say he had found a cabin. We both knew the empty cabin was always there. Let's face it. It was the cabin for those who stood their ground and pestered the hell out of the right person.

Unfortunately, Cathy and I were too brain-dead to move all of our belongings to the new cabin that night.

"No problem," explained our cabin assistant. "Take things you will need in the morning. Then we will bring your luggage to the new cabin some time tomorrow."

After the cabin assistant left, I told Cathy the bad news. Although I rarely took sleeping aids, I had just taken an Advil-PM pill hoping to sleep better, assuming we were staying in our cabin that night.

Cathy said she was very tired and would gladly stay in our cabin until the next morning. Then she fell asleep.

Suddenly, I remembered Cathy's warning. She told me that she didn't snore as long as she had enough rest. Within five minutes, she snored so loud I felt like someone with a megaphone had moved in.

I hoped Cathy would turn onto her side if I approached her slowly. That didn't work. She just shot straight up in bed with the blanket drawn tightly to her chest and began screaming like a Banshee woman.

Deciding to dash into bed, I just made it as she awakened to her own screams. After she calmed down, we had waves of belly laughs about our situation.

Then Cathy fell asleep on her back and snored louder. That's when I decided to go to the new cabin. Before leaving, I called out her name quietly to let her know my new plan.

Once again, she woke up and started screaming. When she finally calmed down, Cathy understood why I was leaving to sleep in the new cabin.

Staggering into the hallway, I held onto the ship's wall railings as the sleeping aid kicked in. At that point, I couldn't remember the number of the new cabin.

Retracing my steps three times, I finally found the door where the new key fit. After it opened, I literally fell into bed.

After we moved into our new cabin the next morning, Cathy had migraine headaches from severe sleep deprivation. That night, I decided to go back to our original cabin in an effort to sleep. That way, Cathy could snore away in peace.

Before leaving, I grabbed my nightgown with a change of clothes for the next day. No matter where I looked, I couldn't find a plastic bag to put them in.

Early the next morning, looking for an elevator back to our new cabin became my focus. I wanted to avoid gossipers who thought carrying my clothes on my arm meant I had spent that night in a man's cabin.

Once again, I couldn't remember the location of our new cabin. Frustrated with the entire fiasco, I took the route of least resistance by attempting to retrace my steps.

That decision cost me a stroll through a long buffet line and a walk around two large swimming pools.

I took what single people refer to as, 'The Walk of Shame.' Laughing to myself, I was amused imagining people were thinking the same thing.

Cathy and I couldn't wait to get off the ship at the end of the cruise. The head honcho offered us $175 in credit. That offer was followed by an additional 15% discount for a future cruise with their fun-filled Carnival cruise line.

After thanking him politely for his offer, I promised myself never to set foot on that ship again.

On the other hand, if he threw in a handsome personal escort, I might have reconsidered.

Flying into Uncertainty
2003

Sleep-deprived, irritable and on people over-load, I dreaded my flight home to Las Vegas.

My friend Rhonda was still asleep in the early morning hours. While wandering around her living room, I looked for a book to ease some of my frustration. The title, *"Embracing Uncertainty"* grabbed my attention immediately.

According to author Susan Jeffers, all of us need to accept what comes in life by looking at disappointing situations as opportunities for positive things to happen. When she used the airport as an example, I imagined my own situation ahead and cringed at the thought of long lines, a flight delay and not getting a front seat for a quick exit.

The author suggested embracing those situations by people-watching, reading a book or meditating. By then I imagined being in a seat with a crying baby behind me. If that happened, forget the author's advice. I would no more be able to watch people or read a book, let alone hypnotize myself into a state of Nirvana bliss.

After arriving at the Los Angeles Airport, I passed through security screening and felt comforted knowing the plane would be on time. As I headed for the boarding gate, the odds were in my favor of actually getting a front seat.

That was an era when Southwest Airlines used a boarding system for passengers based on the order in which they arrived at the gate. After approaching it, I felt relieved seeing only one person standing in line. But then four other people moved into it just seconds later.

Noticing eight bags between them, I wondered if the first four overhead luggage compartments were about to be taken. The author's words came to mind as I tried to accept whatever fate had in store for me.

The four people ahead of me appeared to be a family: a lanky teenage boy, his demure younger sister, and their parents. Dressed in conservative dark clothes, their eyes were bright and they seemed to be open to communicating.

Hearing a foreign language, I approached the young girl hoping she studied English in school and could understand me better than her parents. When the girl's shoulders shrugged with embarrassment, her mother stepped in with a warm smile.

"If you speak more slowly, perhaps I can understand you," she said. When I told her about my concerns, she assured me of her son's help with my luggage when we were boarding the plane.

As the boarding announcement began, her son took my bag and found a space for it in an over-head compartment right over an empty front seat. After I sat down in the seat, he joined his family in the middle of the plane.

A few minutes later, his mother returned and sat in the empty seat next to mine. She was eager to practice her English with me.

"We are from Iran and not planning to return," she explained. "Now we're on our way to Amarillo, Texas to stay with my sister before deciding where to live."

When she told me her husband worked as a goldsmith, I suggested they move to gold-studded Las Vegas. "If your husband worked there, he would probably do very well."

While writing my name, address and phone number on a scrap of paper, she said, "You are beautiful, have great kindness and a special heart."

We talked continuously over the next hour. She was open about their first experience with prejudice after arriving in the United States.

Then she told me about wearing a hijab, her veil. "It is a necessity in Iran and I am relieved of not wearing one here."

She admitted her fear of war and terrorism in Iran. Then she talked about her father who died five months earlier. She imagined how lonely her mother would be without her family nearby.

We laughed about my contentment in not being married. She quickly agreed, "Yes, it is better to be alone, at least until men treat us as equals." We continued talking about the inequality of men and women, stay-at-home moms, and women's independence.

Asking her how to say goodbye in her native language, it seemed ironic when she said, "Salam." How interesting to hear her pronunciation, so much like Israeli people who say, "Shalom." It felt natural to talk easily regardless of our different backgrounds.

When Las Vegas came into view, she asked for help after we landed. They had to change planes and were concerned about finding their next gate. Assuring her of my help, I felt connected to her precious family and wanted to tuck them all under my wing and take them home with me.

After we landed and found their designated gate, her husband asked me to visit with them a little longer. I told him that if my friend weren't waiting outside for me, surely I would have stayed until it was time to go.

A minute later, we heard the boarding announcement. She and I reached out and hugged each other in a tight embrace. We knew our time together was coming to an end. She kissed each of my cheeks and gave me another warm hug.

Then she reached for my right hand and lifted it gently to her sweet, smiling face. As she kissed and caressed the back of my hand, she looked up at me and spoke with loving words in her native language.

At first I felt a pang of discomfort when my imagination took over. *This must be what it would be like to be a queen when someone kissed my hand and then put me on a pedestal, as if I were worthy of living on a higher level in life.*

At that moment, however, a woman with mesmerizing eyes looked at me with gratefulness for something she felt very deeply. Touched by her sincerity, I felt even closer to her. Both of us began to cry as we hugged again. She held me close and long until tears ran down our cheeks.

Exchanging our last emotional words, we wished each other well. I managed to smile and say, "Salam" while waving goodbye.

Walking toward a corner where I would disappear out of sight, I turned around. She was still standing there, waving to me, savoring our last moment until the very end.

After leaving the airport terminal, the author's words surged through me. Having just embraced uncertainty, I knew I had just flown higher than any plane that day.

So Close and Yet So Far
2004

Murphy's Law was in full force when I stayed over-night in Madrid. Being in the right place at the wrong time became a challenge in keeping my wits about me. Although nothing went awry until after the plane landed, Murphy's seed had already been planted in my luggage.

Usually, I packed the same way whether my trips were short or long. I took a small bag on wheels and a large shoulder bag made of light-weight fabric. In the summer months, it was easy to pack light clothing and jelly-roll them into every crevice. By wearing my walking sandals, there was more space for an extra pair and two pair of evening shoes. If the weather turned cool, I wore socks with sandals. If it rained, I stayed indoors or bought a sidewalk umbrella.

Packing lightly also allowed me to carry my bags on the plane, eliminating time at the baggage claim or in the lost luggage office. I always felt good about packing wisely, especially for a woman, as most men would say.

The day before my departure on May 21, 2004, a friend told me that a royal wedding in Madrid was scheduled for the following day. Crown Prince Felipe was marrying Letizia Ortiz, an award-winning journalist and television star. Their wedding reminded me of Monaco's Prince Rainier when he married actress Grace Kelly. Prince Felipe was also marrying a woman without royal blood.

Upon my arrival at the Madrid Airport, I was surprised there were no crowds. Only a few people were waiting for taxi service outside the terminal. After getting into a taxi, I handed my hotel address to the driver as he pulled away from the curb.

Within minutes, it started to drizzle. Then it rained so hard, the driver could barely see through the windshield. The taxi stopped. A police officer approached and motioned him to open the window.

Rain poured in, Spanish words flew, and the driver became upset. He turned to me and attempted to explain their conversation. I couldn't figure out what the driver was saying. I asked the officer if he could speak English.

He turned away and beckoned a policewoman to my window. She explained in broken English that we wouldn't be allowed to travel further. The royal wedding procession was ahead and streets were closed to all traffic. Then I was told to leave the taxi and walk to the hotel.

My mind started clicking. *And just how far was that? A few blocks? Maybe it would be three or four at the most.*

There I stood in the pouring rain, digging out my hooded cotton jacket. Wrestling it on, I walked away from the taxi dragging my luggage behind me. My bags were light, but not water-repellent. Within a few minutes, they had absorbed two pounds of rain between them.

After walking five blocks and turning a corner, I became part of a vast crowd. Everyone was standing behind barricades on both sides of the street. The newlyweds were still scheduled to pass between them within the hour.

Two police officers spotted me as I contemplated my fate in crossing the street. They stopped me with scowls on their faces, insisting I open my luggage immediately. By now my back was aching and my arms felt too weak to do much of anything.

Feeling upset, my mind was resisting. *If they want to see what I've got, they can look for themselves!*

I just shrugged my shoulders and looked bewildered about what they were saying. When they kept pointing to my luggage, I decided to surrender and take on the unavoidable task.

There I stood, unzipping my bag and pulling out my personal things for everyone to see. Pounding rain poured off my face and hands as the officers were dry in their weatherized slickers, hats and boots.

After they realized I was a tourist and not a terrorist, the ordeal was over. Finally satisfied, their faces turned to smiles.

One officer kindly offered to read my internet map in the rain while the ink ran down the page, making it difficult to see the details. He assured me that my hotel was across the street although I still couldn't go there.

Did I understand him correctly?

Unfortunately, I did. There weren't any places to cross the street until the royal procession had passed. He suggested finding a street a few blocks down to get across that way.

First I asked him for the location of the Prada Museum. Going there would be a win-win solution. I could come back after the hoopla ended and finally get to my hotel. No luck. The entire city was shut down with no access to train stations, museums, public buildings, stores, restaurants, or government offices.

Getting out of the rain wasn't possible. Standing under the over-hang of government buildings had been prohibited along that street. No standing, no sitting, nowhere to go except to keep moving. After deciding to walk far enough away from the crowd to look for an opening, four officers stopped me for a bag search.

When it ended and their faces turned to smiles, one officer assured me that crossing any of those streets was prohibited until the procession ended. Joining the crowd to enjoy the royal procession seemed to be the only solution.

Three more policemen spotted me weaving in and out of the crowd as I tried to find an opening along the barricade. They approached me with yet another demand to open my luggage.

At that point, I finally realized how suspicious things looked. I was a hooded person pulling a bag of bombs while wandering around and looking the situation over. That would definitely be a red flag.

Until that moment, I hadn't looked out from under my hood. Otherwise, I would have realized the full extent of security surrounding this now-sacred area.

Police were strategically placed in the street every fifteen feet facing the crowd. Others were scattered behind the crowd. Some rode on horseback while helicopters hovered overhead.

Once again, I passed the test and decided to stay still to avoid drawing any more attention. The pounding rain finally subsided and although I saw an opening along the barricade, I stayed put and looked across the street.

Seven violinists dressed in black tuxedos were protected from the rain under a wide rectangular canopy across the street. They started playing classical Spanish music which could be heard over loudspeakers along the promenade. Their music became the signal for the royal procession to begin after one hour of anticipation.

A black antique car preceded forty horses whose riders were dressed in royal elegance. Behind them, in rows of five, men in blue and red uniforms rode twenty white horses. A second group of men dressed in red and black uniforms rode twenty brown horses strutting in unison.

Then, there they were, the handsome prince and his beautiful new bride. They waved to the applauding crowd from a long, black antique car with large revealing windows. Another car followed behind to signal the end of the pomp and circumstance.

Someone nearby said it could be another hour before the barricade would be taken down. I felt stuck without a place to go.

There wasn't anywhere to sit unless the wet park bench three blocks away appealed to me. By then, I was weary and drenched to the bone. My body refused the thought of sitting on something so cold and damp.

Frustrated and walking in circles, I was filled with indecision and thought about what to do next. That was taken care of as five police officers approached me with a very thorough inspection of my bags.

One of them took on the investigation by reaching deeply into my bag on wheels. He pulled out my zip-lock bag of 200 vitamin pills, enough for my five-week vacation. As the pills raised suspicion, three other officers surrounded me.

When the first policeman lifted another plastic bag into the air filled with 40 calcium pills, the suspense heightened. At that point, they considered me a drug dealer. Four officers on horseback joined the circle from behind.

Now I definitely had some fast talking to do. Speaking in broken Spanish and French with an extra measure of pantomime seemed like a reasonable idea. I began imitating someone taking vitamins by placing imaginary pills on my tongue and swallowing them with a glass of make-believe water. When the policewomen started smiling, everyone looked satisfied. After a short huddled conference, they asked me to move on.

Leaving quickly, I headed in the opposite direction to look for any place to park my tired body and mind. After spotting an open tourist office, I dragged my luggage up two flights of stairs and asked the man behind the counter about sitting inside for a while.

His answer defeated me. "I'm sorry, not today."

That did it. I walked down the stairs and took out my deflated exercise ball. After placing it on the bottom step, I was more than willing to sit on it. As my eyes closed, I drifted off to sleep.

At some point, a sudden burst of sunshine awakened me. Seeing people wandering about freely, I gathered my things, walked across the street to my hotel and stumbled into the lobby. After the clerk led me to my room, I fell asleep as my head touched the pillow.

Two hours later, I woke up feeling famished. Restaurants were still closed until eight o'clock. Watching television could be interesting if there were English-speaking channels with news about the wedding.

Although I only saw a fraction of the festivities, the entire affair stirred my curiosity. No luck. Every channel was consumed with coverage of the royal wedding exclusively in Spanish.

After landing in Paris the next day, I found out why extensive security coverage had been provided before and after the newlyweds came through the city streets. Two months earlier, a terrorist bombing in the Madrid train station had killed 190 people.

The Spanish government raised the possibility of another bombing the day before the wedding. That's why F-18 jets were provided to patrol the skies around the Prado palace to protect 400 dinner guests, including Prince Charles, President Nelson Mandela, and King Abudullah. On the day of the wedding, NATO provided surveillance around Almudena Cathedral during the ceremony.

When the royal couple left the cathedral, they were protected with heavy security as they moved slowly through the crowded streets. At that moment, I realized the driving rain and a potential bombing couldn't keep over one million people from cheering and waving to the royal couple.

Finally understanding what the bride had endured, I knew my short hours of discomfort were nothing compared to hers. She had just made a life-long commitment to live under the scrutiny of the police, to smile for all the photographers, and perform traditional ceremonies that would have bored me silly.

By then, it was pretty obvious. I definitely had the better end of the deal.

When You Need to Get Out of Town
2004

Many people dream of going to Paris. That's why it sounded strange when I heard Parisians say they wanted to go to Corsica. I over-heard someone say she absolutely needed to get out of town.

Like many people who vacationed in Corsica, it was a welcome change from city buildings and sidewalks. It reminded me of people in New York City who went to the beach or away to the Catskill Mountains for the same reasons.

After my over-night stay in Madrid, I flew into Charles de Gaulle Airport in Paris. When Michelle and Charles met me there, we boarded a plane to Corsica. They had already made previous plans to stay in their five-bedroom vacation home for several days.

During her stay with me in Las Vegas, I only knew Michelle as a painter. In Corsica, I came to know her as a mother and homemaker when her twin daughters came to visit.

A few days later, her sister and close friends flew in to join them. Michelle cooked and baked for her family and friends, totaling nine at one sitting. I saw the tireless energy of a sixty-year old woman who had more spunk than most people in their thirties. She scrubbed terrace tiles, kitchen floors, and the face of her granddaughter. For me, it was pure joy to be part of a close-knit French family. They sang, laughed, and with raised hands, exclaimed, "Ooopah!" That's how they expressed praise to those who made other dishes with dinner each night.

Everywhere we went, Corsica's diverse island beauty surrounded us. The island was everything rolled into one: turquoise water, white sandy beaches and steep mountain cliffs.

One day, the three of us toured the town of Bonifacio where an original military fort had been built hundreds of feet above the sea. Accessible only through a drawbridge, the fort was used while making the movie, *"The Guns of Navarone."*

Later that day, Charles drove us into pine-studded mountains 6,000 feet high. We had lunch in a magnificent outdoor café while watching the industrious mountain-climbing enthusiasts who had replaced dedicated skiers just a week ago.

Snow was melting at the highest elevation of 7,000 feet where the rugged terrain reminded me of the Grand Tetons. Mountain water flowed as its waterfalls turned into streams. They wound through pastures, cascaded over rocks and finally flowed right out to sea.

Major tourist attractions focused on Corsica's restaurants. Some were perched over the sea along 300-foot high cliffs. Aside from the mountain café 6,000 feet up, there were restaurants along the beach. They were built on decks where women sunbathed in the semi-nude.

Two days before we left for Paris, I learned about Corsica's two different faces. Charles told me about the native Corsicans of Mafia legend. They protected their land dearly. Stores in every Corsican town had an exclusive array of knives to suit the needs of those dealing in that business.

Confidently armed, they persuaded foreigners to go elsewhere when mention was made about opening a new business. If taxes were excessive, it was impossible for foreigners to show a profit. If the taxes weren't paid, their properties were taken away or their businesses were bombed.

One afternoon, we drove past the remains of a nightclub on the beach. After the owner refused to close it, an empty space took its place. It had been bombed by those Corsicans who didn't want a competitor.

It's too bad the owner didn't leave sooner. He definitely needed to get out of town.

Downtown to Uptown in One Fell Swoop
2004

When Michelle, Charles and I flew back from Corsica, spring time in Paris took my breath away.

A few days later, Michelle invited me to her friend's photography exhibit. It was actually in his art studio which took up a large area of his apartment.

On the night of the exhibit, Michelle parked her car in front of his building. It looked like a throw-back from the Bohemian era of the 60's. In her limited broken English, Michelle told me homeless people had lived there until two years ago when it finally became a desirable place to live.

We entered the building through a wannabe lobby. Graffiti filled the interior walls of what looked like a dark basement. Mailboxes, doors and ceiling pipes were covered with it. To top off the scene, an emaciated dog with his head hung low was limping through the dark, eerie hallway.

Michelle's friend was a set decorator by trade. Although still struggling as a professional photographer, he knew the importance of promotion. He asked two friends to share the exhibit and invite people they knew to attend.

Frankly, I couldn't fathom what any of the photographs were all about. In my opinion, it took a lot of guts to hang them up, let alone ask hundreds of dollars for them. I did, however, appreciate the photographers' laid-back attitudes. At least they waited for people to ask about buying their pictures.

Most of the attendees were in their twenties and thirties. Some wandered from room to room. Others sat at tables with flickering candles under dimmed ceiling lights.

Several people who held hand-rolled cigarettes stood near a display of three photographs: a man's bare stomach, left hip and lower thigh. All the photographs were over-exposed. To me, they looked like mistakes someone forgot to throw away.

I followed a few people into the kitchen for a snack. An array of peanuts, trail mix, breads and cheeses offered tasty choices on a long counter. My mouth watered when I saw a vegetable quiche on a wooden board. In the middle of the counter, an entire pig's leg stood upright. It was thoroughly cooked and tied by leather straps for people to easily cut away what they wanted.

Frankly, that sight took my appetite away. I decided to tag along with a small group of folks in their seventies who had just arrived. Dressed in clothes from the Bohemian era, they were people who probably had the most money to spend.

Everyone headed for a display I hadn't seen yet. They looked at the first five photographs which were skeletons of a baby's head. After a short discussion, they looked at a picture of four badly bruised forearms tied to a black metal bar.

Moving on, they were amused by the last photograph of a man in a business suit. He was standing in an art gallery with nothing on display. The man was just looking at a light bulb hanging on a cord in the middle of an empty wall.

Questioning myself, I wondered what was happening. *Am I missing something here?*

People thought those photographs were imaginative and thought-provoking. Well, they were. So after my thoughts were provoked, I left the room and happily spotted Michelle saying goodbye to her friend. That was the highlight of my experience at the exhibit.

A week later, I watched Michelle finish an outdoor painting of a magnificent structure which housed hundreds of botanicals. Built in1626, it was the major attraction in Jardin de Plantes, the oldest gardens in France.

After Michelle put her paints away, she said we were going to attend an art exhibit. I looked like a hippie in overalls and sandals. We both looked scruffy. She didn't care about her paint-streaked hands and off we went.

The exhibit took place in the main office building of the Colas Foundation which was located in a posh area of Paris. As one of three largest development companies, it was contracted to build the city roads and bridges.

Every year, the Colas foundation purchased paintings which reflected the contemporary trends in roads for the future. The artwork was then offered for sale during cocktail parties in the lobby. Those not sold were hung in other offices around the world.

Michelle was one of twenty artists selected for exhibit in 2003, which gave her entry as an invited guest in 2004.

More than one-hundred people attended the affair. Men wore conservative business suits and gathered in small groups to chat. Throughout the lobby, women walked elegantly in dresses, shoes and hats in the highest fashions. I enjoyed wearing my casual clothes without a care about making a good impression. Thankfully, I gave up that burden thirty years ago.

Many guests enjoyed champagne on the terrace served by men in white jackets and black ties. I headed for the exhibit area where pastries topped with caviar, salmon hors' d'oeuvres and fine French chocolates were being offered.

A French woman stood next to me and made a comment about the scrumptious appetizers. When I told her I was an American who spoke very little French, she began speaking in English.

After pulling out a flyer from her bag, she told me about her sculptures. While encouraging me to contact her, she then pointed to her website on the reverse side of her flyer.

Taken aback by her aggressive marketing approach, I realized the difference between her and those struggling photographers. It really didn't matter to her that this was an Upper Crust event. The woman had a lot of crust.

Come Again?
2004

When I introduced Michelle to Zoe, the two artists hit it off right away. Then, after a short conversation, Michelle invited Zoe to her home.

Four days later, when Charles joined all of us at the dinner table, Michelle was telling Zoe about our interesting art gallery experience the other night.

She explained that while she and I walked past art galleries in their favorite art district, Charles walked ahead of us less than a block away. At one point, Michelle wanted me to look into a particular gallery window. As she pointed to a painting by an American artist, I told her it wasn't easy for me to see past the crowded window.

When we came to another gallery window, Michelle pointed to another painting by the same artist. She was convinced I would recognize him. Unfortunately, I couldn't see much behind that gallery window either. It displayed too many large paintings to see much of anything smaller.

Since the galleries were closed, we weren't able to solve the mystery. Michelle was a little frustrated. She couldn't understand how I didn't know the name of the famous American painter, Hondy Rarl.

Frustrated and laughing at the same time, Michelle caught up with Charles to straighten things out. She told him how surprised she was about my lack of knowledge, especially since I was familiar with many other painters. Charles couldn't believe it either. How come I did not know the name of such a famous American painter?

Suddenly, a painting caught his eye in the window of another gallery. Pointing to it, he said, "There's one of his paintings. Can you see it?" Bursting into laughter, I realized what had happened.

It wasn't my complete ignorance after all. The issue was their difficult pronunciation of Andy Warhol.

The next evening, Michelle shared the story with her daughters. They also had a hard time saying Andy Warhol's name.

It was a night of uproarious laughter which started an avalanche of mispronounced English words spoken by the average French person. Since their language didn't use some of our American sounds, it made sense that their tongues were only trained for pronouncing French words.

For instance, French people find it difficult to pronounce the 'R' and 'L' sounds in words such as 'squirrel' and 'scroll.' Those were the two reasons they couldn't say, 'Warhol.' They looked and sounded like they were trying to control a bunch of marbles in their mouths.

Then there's the word, 'south,' or any word with the sound 'th.' Everyone was capable of letting their tongues make the 'th' sound. However, after they put their tongues out past their teeth, everything stopped moving.

Everyone looked like they forgot the back-up plan for retrieving their tongues. Slowly and with silly grins, they pulled them back in long enough to try again.

By then, it was their turn to challenge me. It was comparable to the famous American tongue-twister, "How much wood could a woodchuck chuck if a woodchuck could chuck wood?"

Although I had studied French in high school for three years, it meant nothing forty years later when I was facing French people. Everyone had a great time hearing me mess up royally.

At that point, I considered telling them it wasn't a fair match of tongues. Frankly, I'd rather have marbles in my mouth instead of my foot.

A Piece of the Action
2004

The night before leaving Las Vegas for the summer, I listened to the Jay Leno show. At one point, he talked about the 1944 invasion of Normandy when America freed France from German occupation. Leno said a recent poll claimed that 43% of French citizens didn't know about the Normandy invasion.

The audience laughed at Jay's comment. I didn't know what to think until I was in Paris on the sixth of June during France's 60th year celebration. Until then, I wasn't aware of how intensely France honored those war efforts.

The celebration lasted two days. Activities were continuously televised throughout those nights. Interviews of war veterans from France, the United States and Germany spoke about how all sides had suffered. Excerpts from war footage were shown as well as several scenes from the movie, *"Saving Private Ryan."*

During those two days, Paris was jammed with traffic. The road to Normandy had been closed an hour away. Parachutes tossed rose petals into the sea to represent those who had died.

Before the D-Day ceremonies, I met Michelle's friend, Catherine. She was a research pharmacist who worked with Dr. Edouard Sakiz, the man who created the abortion pill.

The doctor considered Catherine his right arm. She was also the only woman ever appointed to such a high position in a world of male dominance.

The next day, Michelle and I met them at the doctor's office before we all had lunch together. While waiting for Dr. Sakiz, I read a magazine article about his revolutionary accomplishments.

I also learned about the pressures he survived from developing the abortion pill. He was being squeezed by the Pro-Lifers who tried to boycott his product if he kept it **on** the market, while the abortionist group pressured him if he took it **off** the market. His home had been vandalized with vicious words, referring to the doctor as a baby-killer.

Regardless of one's beliefs about abortion, this man's dedication to helping women at a dangerous time in history deserved respect. When Bill Clinton was president, Dr. Sakiz told him he would give the United States the rights to the pill despite the patent. Although President Clinton wanted the pill, Congressmen from the Bush era fought against it.

We bought what we needed from the Chinese. They illegally copied the doctor's original formula and then disregarded patent agreements. Since then, Chinese companies were cited for contaminated products.

When I asked Dr. Sakiz why he didn't pursue the United States market, he said it wasn't worth the fight to bring his pill to our country any more. The cost became too high. Aside from that, it was difficult to reverse the stigma and recover from a black-eye when there had been enormous negative publicity.

As a doctor and scientist, his major focus had not been on making huge profits. Dr. Sakiz just wanted to offer women an alternative method to poorly performed surgical procedures. Even if we had continued to purchase the pill from China, he was satisfied knowing women now had a choice.

When our car pulled up to a posh restaurant on that hot day in Paris, Dr. Sakiz was dressed meticulously in a suit and tie. He insisted on opening the door for me when the doorman could have easily helped me out of the car.

He and I sat together during lunch. We also dined with Catherine's godson, a 22-year old student engineer who had a great future ahead of him.

Turning to Dr. Sakiz, I asked if he would like to be that age again. As a 78-year old man, he answered, "Being that age is too young. I would like to be forty again."

I was curious about why he thought being forty was better. Looking at me with a twinkle in his bright blue eyes, he poked my arm gently and laughed.

"That was the age when we began to know the real truths about life, eh?" I certainly agreed with him.

Dr. Sakiz was voted "Feminist of the Year" by "The Feminist Majority Foundation." He and Catherine were invited to attend the D-Day ceremonies to meet with other dignitaries who were also known for helping women.

That time was more than marking the day Americans helped liberate the French. To me, it also included the celebration of the French doctor who liberated women around the world.

What I Won't Miss about Paris
2004

Apartment Bathrooms:

The floor space in many apartment bathrooms was usually taken up with drying racks in the middle of the room. There weren't any clothes dryers. Electricity costs were usually around $1,200 a month.

That made me think about life before electric dryers were invented. People hung laundry outside a window or on a clothes line. Everything smelled fresh in the country air. Having been a farm girl, I can attest to that.

Aside from the limited floor space, moving around in those bathrooms wasn't easy, especially when I tried to make my way to the sink or into the bath tub.

Most bath tubs had neither shower curtains nor sliding glass doors. If shower sprayers weren't attached to the wall, taking a shower became an interesting challenge.

By first grasping a hand-held sprayer in one hand, I washed with the other hand while trying to avoid spraying water all over the floor. A huge mirror on the wall in front of the tub was positioned perfectly. That way, I could easily see the ridiculous positions my body made while trying to maneuver the sprayer.

Toilets:

Most toilets in apartment bathrooms were in narrow spaces with sliding doors or doors on hinges. Reaching for the toilet paper posed other issues. The rolls were usually placed on a short, vertical pole near the toilet. There wasn't room to put a roll on the wall near the toilet. I wouldn't have been able to grab it anyway. There wasn't any room to bend my elbow.

Toilet Flushers:

Locating toilet flushers in apartment bathrooms presented other challenges. When the flusher was on the floor, I had to decide whether to step on the flusher or push it with my fingers.

There were times when the flusher was above the toilet where the water tank would usually be positioned. Most often the water tank was suspended overhead. It became impossible to reach if the toilet had stopped working.

That's what happened the day Charles, Michelle and I flew back from Corsica. Charles climbed up to the water tank to put water in it, thereby allowing gravity to pull the flusher down so the toilet would be able to flush.

Some flushers were attached to the water tank and fixed to a gear shift doohickey. In those situations my brain was totally confused. *Should I pull the lever toward myself or push it in against the tank?*

Making the wrong decision would loosen the gear shift. That's when the entire water tank could also fly off the toilet.

Within a few weeks, I saw every imaginable toilet flusher. By then I considered myself an expert. That was a very rewarding feeling, especially since I never thought of myself as an expert on anything else in Paris.

Apartment Elevators:

Many apartment elevators in Paris were like those in Italy, old and tiny. They were also barely three feet square. My challenge was in figuring out how to get into them.

The first time I approached one, I faced a large metal door. After pulling the door open toward me, two louvered doors became my next challenge. The ultimate task was in holding the outside door open while pushing the two louvered doors inward.

If those doors didn't fold in the middle, I wouldn't have been able to get into the elevator. Pulling my suitcases into the elevator made it more difficult. One might think I could have asked someone to help me. Forget about that. There wasn't room for anyone else in the elevator.

Traffic:

During my visits in Paris, I never considered driving there. Sitting in a moving car was a hazard in itself. Most of the time, I held onto my seat for dear life.

People drove very fast in Paris. Many drivers barely squeezed by on narrow streets. They also appeared confused about where they were going.

Huge roundabouts presented the worst situations. Most often, there were eight possible ways to enter or exit roundabouts with no demarcations on the road. Whoever felt so inclined to go first was the person who got ahead.

Those drivers needed good peripheral vision when cars came at them from every angle. Many cars came from the left and passed in front of everyone as they exited on the right. Putting a mix of eager motorcyclists in the mix topped off perhaps the craziest traffic on the planet.

The near-misses were usually followed by hand-slapping gestures on the steering wheels from drivers who were cut off. Despite all of that, the sound of honking horns was rare.

A year ago, the government passed a law prohibiting people from driving too fast. Since fast drivers always tested the limits, they still drove like bats out of hell.

Don't Moose around with Me
2005

After six delightful experiences in my travel club, the seventh one proved to be the makings of a very uncomfortable, but now, funny story.

In the past I had only good things to say about club members. It was easy to be among strangers who were wonderful from the time they opened the door and welcomed me in. Their homes were cheery and met every accommodation required.

Dora was a retired Mormon nurse who was born in Finland and moved to Seattle thirty years ago. When we spoke on the phone, she sounded as sweet as all the other widowed or single women in the travel club.

She grew her own organic vegetable garden and focused on healthy living. Dora was willing to extend the usual three-day travel club stay to a time frame that suited me. We agreed that I would stay for two months.

A week before I arrived, Dora told me she had a permanent renter who lived upstairs and used the guest bathroom. She quickly assured me about my private bedroom downstairs which would be the coolest room during the occasional 90-degree days.

After arriving, I was surprised when Dora took me to my room. It was actually part of a basement full of patio furniture and her grandchildren's toys. At one time, it had been a family room with a fireplace.

Dora said it was a bedroom, but there weren't any closets. She pointed to a coat rack to hang my clothes and a dresser with two drawers for everything else.

My double bed was pushed into a corner. It was perpendicular to the fireplace wall. That meant I had only one way to get into my bed easily.

A moose head hung over the fireplace. Another moose head hung on the wall to my right. I asked Dora why straw hats were on its antlers.

"That's so you don't hurt yourself getting into bed," she replied seriously.

Although it made sense to her, she didn't take into account the fact that I didn't want a moose head next to me all night.

"Another person was upset about that, too," she said with a smile. "He said he couldn't sleep all night thinking about the moose staring at him." I knew what he was feeling.

When I got into bed, the moose's left eye stared directly in line with mine. If I turned my head to the right, there he was, staring at me sideways with his black, cue-ball eye.

After asking Dora if she could remove the moose heads, she had a problem with that. I decided to take them down or cover them up with the blankets covering her patio furniture.

The moose near my head wouldn't budge, but I was able to take down the one over the fireplace. It took two blankets to cover up most of it. After pushing the head behind the patio furniture, I finally had one less moose in my life.

Using one large blanket, I was able to cover up the antlers, face and neck of the moose next to my bed. After I finished draping him, his straw-hat antlers were still reigning over his masked face.

That scene didn't look any more bizarre with or without his masked face. Finally realizing my fate, I settled for the moose as my nightly companion.

The private bathroom turned out to be one bathroom divided into three unrelated areas. The toilet was near the stairs in the hallway behind the hot water heater. The shower was in a room near the sauna but without a sink in sight.

The next day, I asked Dora about a sink. "That's in the hallway," she said. "It's located between the washing machine and the toilet."

Using that sink wouldn't do. There wasn't any light to see anything and no mirror in case I wanted to see something. She decided to offer me the guest bathroom so I could watch myself put on makeup.

"The shower in that bathroom is broken," she explained. "So you will have to use the shower near the sauna downstairs. The renter and other travel club members use that one, too. When I have nothing available, I put them on the sauna benches or on the living room floor upstairs."

That's when I knew Dora was running a small boarding house. It took two weeks to find another travel club member who was available for guests.

After moving out of Dora's house, I called the travel club secretary. She promptly terminated Dora's membership since someone else had reported her for the same reason.

The club rules included termination if two people had the same complaint. That made sense. In this case, being stared down by a moose was definitely a deal breaker.

Gems in the Emerald City
2005

The first time I saw San Francisco, it seemed to have all the things a city could offer. After I saw Seattle, however, that's where I left my heart.

It's no wonder Seattle was a shoo-in for me. As a devout tree lover, I was overwhelmed with its 6,000 acres of city parks and lush green forests. That's why it's called, "The Emerald City."

Sure, it rains a lot there. However, someone told me it didn't rain as much as it did in San Francisco and Portland. Certainly there are over-cast and wet days there, but New Englanders say Seattle usually gets misty or just drizzles. Although it pours like cats and dogs on the east coast, you can count on one hand the number of days it rains like that in Seattle.

During my life, I've been caught in a deluge, but walking in a light Seattle mist is delightfully different. Health-wise, the moisture is good for our hair and skin. It's also a perfect time to inhale the fragrances of nature, like the smell of freshly cut grass.

Aside from bicycle paths weaving throughout the city, there are parks in unusual places. For instance, Freeway Park is a small area perched above a freeway overpass in the downtown area. Drivers can look up at its retaining walls and admire the profusion of vines cascading over them. It just warmed my heart knowing Freeway Park was created for people who wanted more trees and greenery wherever imaginable.

The spice of life brims over in Green Lake Park where its center of attention is Green Lake. Trees, bushes and grasses hang on every crevice along the lake's edge. Tips of arched willow tree branches bend gracefully into the water. Large platforms float further out where diving boards toss kids into the water. Seattle's national boat races are held there. People rent kayaks, row boats and paddle boats but nothing motorized is allowed in the water.

A whole other life surrounds the no-litter-anywhere park. There's live theater, areas for sports, a pitch and putt golf course, and a playground with a wading pool for the kiddies.

Surrounded almost entirely by huge trees, charming older homes are hidden deep in the hilltops. Aside from neighborhood stores and shops, there are restaurants with outdoor seating facing the lake.

The three-mile walking path around the perimeter of Green Lake is the common thread pulling everyone together. Moving counter-clockwise, the outside lane provides passage for bicycles, roller blades and skateboards. The inside lane is for those who want to walk, jog or push a stroller. From infants to folks in their eighties, the path is chock-full of every ethnicity and lifestyle. This is Americana in all its glory.

Before six in the morning, very few people walk the lake. After working hours, over 200 people passed me in fifteen minutes. These were nature lovers as well as fitness-conscious folks. Women out-numbered men, but not by much. Most men whizzed past others on roller skates or jogged with their dogs on a leash. Other men walked with women or pushed a baby carriage. Women walked alone or jogged with friends. Every tenth person walked a dog. Every twentieth person walked two dogs. One day, I saw a woman pushing her dog in a stroller.

Green Lake is over 100 years old. I wondered how much had changed after all those years. Back then, jogging was probably called 'running' and people didn't wear brightly-colored outfits with designer labels. Men with muscular chests and abs didn't run without a shirt either. People weren't distracted with Bluetooth wireless headsets and misconstrued as crazy people talking to themselves. There were no dangling IPod wires and nothing plugged up their ears to take them away from the delightful sounds of the lake.

People didn't have multi-colored hair back then. No one had a ring hanging from an eyebrow, a nose or an exposed belly button. People weren't dancing on roller blades or cruising on skateboards. There weren't any Seattle Freedom Skaters back then either. No one dared to roller skate in the nude at midnight when the coast was clear like they did nowadays.

Although things have changed over the years, some people still walked the lake for its camaraderie. Many old-timers were attached to the lake for sentimental reasons. Some of them sat for hours at the concession stand where espresso, ices and pretzels were sold.

One day I stopped to talk with three of them about the lure of the lake. "There's a lot of history for some people here," a retired home appraiser explained. "Many people have been walking Green Lake for what seems like a lifetime. They walked with their spouses when they were still alive and they still come here for the connection they hold dearly."

Another man told me about the romantic attachment the younger generation had for the lake. Hearing about two of the many engagements there, I was surprised and touched.

One of my favorites was the story about a man who proposed to his girlfriend by putting up signs along the entire three-mile walking path. After placing the signs, he hid behind a building near the spot where she finished her daily walks. As his girlfriend started her walk and saw the signs, she never thought they were there for her. Then, as she read the last one, her boyfriend came out of hiding. He kneeled down on one knee and asked, "Will you marry me?"

Another favorite story came from Tim, the man who ran the concession stand. His story impressed me since the plan involved other people, all complete strangers.

A young man wanted to surprise his girlfriend with two dozen roses. After buying the flowers, he went to the opposite side of the lake to the place where she always started her daily walk in the clockwise lane.

Roses in hand, he approached twenty-three strangers who were walking counter-clockwise. Showing them a photograph of his girlfriend, he asked, "Will you please give this rose to her as you pass each other?"

Everyone gladly agreed to help him out. Each person handed her a rose without any explanation and continued walking.

When she came around the bend and saw her boyfriend standing in the middle of the path, he presented her with the twenty-fourth rose and asked her to marry him.

Seattle newspapers covered the first engagement story. Both stories impacted people years later. Although everyone knew each woman received diamonds that day, the real gems were the men who made those moments priceless.

Canada through Different Eyes
2007

Jean and I met through our travel club last summer. I spent one week in her Seattle home where I had my own bedroom downstairs. This year we had planned a road trip through the Canadian Rockies.

A few weeks before our trip, I became concerned about Jean's sleeping habits. In the three nights ahead, we were scheduled to stay with other members of our club. It would be the first time Jean and I had to share a bed.

Since I had been sleeping alone for many years, sharing a room with someone, let alone a bed, made me a little uneasy. Getting five to six hours of sleep under my belt was considered a good night's sleep. I wondered if that was going to change.

Before we planned our trip, I asked Jean if she snored. She was confident that she didn't. "I don't think I snore, but if I do, just poke me and I'll roll over. Or let me know and I'll stop."

We stayed in Kamloops the first day after crossing the Canadian border. Our travel club hosts also used their home as a beautiful bed and breakfast. Fortunately, we had separate living quarters with our queen-sized bed. If Jean snored, I was ready to sleep on the living room couch.

When Jean fell asleep, it became obvious that she was an avid snorer. Imagining she was like most people who snored, Jean couldn't be stopped easily.

After tapping her gently, shaking the bed and poking her, nothing worked. That's not to say she didn't stop at all. She gave me a few peaceful moments. They just didn't last long.

It seems to me that people who **don't** snore are usually light sleepers, whereas people who **do** snore can sleep through an earthquake. At one point, Jean said she slept through an earthquake. My case rests.

The next day, we headed further north. When we stopped to eat, I had a conversation with an interesting man. He said Canadians were steeped in the history of their country as well as our own part of the Americas. He told me about the first people who set foot on our continent. When I was growing up, all of us referred to them as 'Indians.' Canadians refer to them as 'The First Nation People."

"Think of that," he explained. "Indians are from India and Americans are people like you who were born in America." That sure made a lot of sense.

I just love Canadians. Sometimes I wonder if they were born smiling. Whether it was the person in a toll booth or someone behind a cash register, there were usually smiles coming my way.

Canadians were dedicated and courteous people as well. They reminded me of Italians, another friendly group always willing to go out of their way whenever I asked for directions. They all stopped what they were doing, got into their cars and showed me exactly where I needed to go.

Unfortunately, exploring Canada had its sad moments when we saw the effects of global warming. Through the lower mountain elevations, millions of pine trees were dying. They were cast in a deep red-brown across the mountains as they wasted away.

Our earth wasn't getting cold enough in the winter anymore. The pine beetles that would have frozen to death were now alive in the spring and creating havoc.

Someone told me that people who owned houses in those areas paid $3,500 to remove each dead tree threatening to fall on their homes. The cost of removing a tree used to be $700. Someone else said the government was at a stand-still about how to deal with the enormous cost of removing trees in their national parks.

I was ready for some mental sunshine. Jean parked her car in Banff National Park where we walked along a forest trail. When we came to the end of it, we were standing in front of Lake Louise. To me, it looked like an awesome, three-dimensional painting.

Since meeting and traveling together, I came to know Jean's personality traits. She didn't react to things quite like I did. She appreciated the beauty of Lake Louise, but Jean didn't have the desire to express it.

Although I certainly respect people like Jean, there are times when I like to be with someone who shares my excitement. Being with Jean was like telling a really funny joke and the other person barely reacts.

However, Jean did make a comment when she saw the color of the water in Lake Louise. People said I would be surprised when I saw how blue the water appeared in the lake.

I wondered if they meant it was like Oregon's Crater Lake. Its water was a deep crystal clear blue. I could see as far down as my eye would take me. It looked like a mirror whose mountains and trees cast their reflection on its surface.

Lake Louise wasn't like that at all. It was an unusual blue. The color wasn't a deep blue, nor was it easy to see through. It was actually a light shade of aqua, as if skim milk had been poured into the water.

It also held a reflection of the sun and the glare from Mount Victoria's glaciers. Flanked by two fjords, the lake spilled over smack dab in front of us.

Without food since breakfast, we headed for the dining room in the Fairmont Chateau Lake Louise Hotel. The century-old hotel was built facing the lake. Like other resort hotels, it offered a dining experience in which paying for the ambiance was expected. The Fairmont Chateau Hotel was pure elegance. Our experience was well worth twice the price. While eating our lunch, we had the pleasure of looking at the magnificent scenery, until it started to rain. That's when everything fogged over.

After deciding to leave Lake Louise and the fog behind, we drove through pouring rain or walked through it in a quick tour of Banff. Then we decided to return when the sky was clear so we could experience Banff and Lake Louise from a dry perspective.

Three days later, we returned to the lake around noon. Jean wanted to eat in the deli where the food was less expensive and the ambiance was limited. I was glad the hotel provided an eatery with a view for folks who might be on a budget. The view of the lake could still be seen sideways if people sat on the ledged-seating along the windows.

Before we made our way to the hotel, I heard a familiar voice. It sounded just like Jim Carrey giving a lecture about the lake. When I turned around, I saw a man who had Jim Carrey's build and could actually have been his brother.

Although Jean was hungry and wanted to get something to eat, I wasn't about to miss that for anything. I suggested she go ahead without me. We had always agreed that neither of us would miss out on anything the other person had no interest in experiencing.

After Jean decided to stay, she was glad she did. The mountain guide who gave the lecture worked for the hotel and climbed those mountains on his days off. Certainly any guide would have provided us with a thorough understanding about the famous area, but it was this particular guide who made it memorable.

He had Jim Carrey's voice and expressions down pat, right down to his animated facial contortions and that devilish grin around his over-sized teeth. It was reminiscent of his colorful film character in the movie, *"The Mask."*

First he wanted to impress us with Mount Victoria. As he turned toward the mountain, he asked, "How high do you think Mount Victoria is from this view?"

Someone suggested it couldn't be more than 500 feet high. With the wave of his hand in a humorous Jim Carrey gesture, he whipped out a photo of the Empire State Building and asked, "Do you think it's as tall as this building?"

The thought seemed ridiculous. That's when he revealed four more of the same photos. They were attached to one another, unfolding vertically before us.

"If you put four of these buildings on top of each other, then you would know approximately how high Mount Victoria really is," he said.

We were stunned to say the least. He had that great Jim Carrey 'fooled ya' look when he saw our reactions. Then he asked us another question.

"How far do you think Mount Victoria is from where we are standing?"

It seemed to be just a stone's throw away. He was just laying low, ready to fool us again.

"Now you know what an illusion all of this is," he said. "I know the lake looks very close to Mount Victoria, but it's really five miles from where you're standing. I just thought I would mention that in case you wanted to take a walk around the lake. I hear people all the time who start out with that in mind, thinking it will only take a few minutes."

He pointed to a spot barely around the corner. "See? That's where you would be in ten minutes."

Then he told us about his adventures climbing mountains that were similar to Mount Victoria, which rose over two miles at its highest point. "When the hotel celebrated its 100th anniversary, I climbed to the top of that mountain over there," he said. "This was the photo taken when I reached the top."

He took us in front of the small statue of a man looking out toward the mountains. As he stood beside the statue, he asked us to look closely.

"See? I looked like this fella right here. That's how it was 100 years ago when Swiss climbers wore knickers and used a stick for climbing. He was the first man who climbed the mountain and he was wearing an outfit just like mine."

I looked at the statue of the guide with his hand over his brow. He looked like Jim Carrey in one of his humorous stunts.

When the guide got our attention again, he had an interesting rhetorical question. "Why would the Swiss and the Germans come all the way over here when they have so many Alps to look at in their own country?"

All of us were puzzled and had no answer. He paused, looking first at us, then sideways to the mountains, and then back at us with a typical Jim Carrey beady-eyed stare. I figured he was just waiting to pounce on us with the answer.

"Their Alps are surrounded by farmlands and towns, but there's no wilderness like this. So people come here to see the grizzlies, wolverines, lynx and cougars. It is the only place in North America that still exists like that. There are no more grizzlies in California although the grizzly is its state animal. How sad is that?"

After the lecture was over, I asked the Jim Carrey look-alike if people told him how much he looked like his brother.

"All the time," he answered. "Besides, he **is** my brother. He's a Canadian, you know." Then he smiled and walked away in that Jim Carrey gait.

Like I said before, I just love Canadians.

Only the Nose Knows
2007

By the time Jean and I arrived in Calgary, Peter and Janet were welcome sights as our travel club hosts. Janet opened the door with the warmest smile and biggest hug anyone could bestow on a weary traveler.

Once again, Jean and I shared a queen-sized bed. My eye was already on the couch downstairs, just in case the ear plugs I had purchased didn't work. Since Janet snored, Peter offered similar ear plugs made of foam which he claimed to be the best. For better comfort and placement, he suggested wetting their tips before placing them in my ears.

When the ear plugs worked, I was thrilled. Adjusting to the sound of my own breathing, however, was a different story. Wearing them made me feel like I was scuba diving. After a while, I considered taking the plugs out.

As I looked over at Jean in the dim light from the window, she seemed to be sleeping soundly and had miraculously stopped snoring. Removing my ear plug closest to her mouth, I wanted to see if Jean was really snore-free.

That's when I heard the loudest snoring sound imaginable. It felt like a deeply embedded organism blasting its way through every crevice of my ear canal. Stuffing the plug back into my ear, I quickly avoided another blast with megaphone force.

As the night wore on, trying to adjust to something shoved into my ears didn't work. Although I moved my pillow and head from side to side, I couldn't find a comfortable place.

While watching Jean sleeping so peacefully, I asked myself a question. *How can she sleep through all of this, while I'm awake all night?*

At that point, I wanted to awaken her just to tell her how miserable I was. But then my feelings changed knowing it wasn't her fault.

The next morning, Jean was still unaware of my predicament and desperate need for sleep. I've been told that many people who snore actually deny it. They flat out refuse to believe they snore at all. Many challenge their loved ones to record them in the middle of the night, as if they needed proof.

Perhaps they can't face being responsible for another person's discomfort. I could relate to that. After all, a simple operation would fix the problem. Then both people could get a good night's sleep. It seemed like a common sense thing to do.

Then again, I can understand avoiding an operation and putting one's head in the ground like an ostrich. Maybe that's why mates don't complain. They just make the sacrifice of wearing ear plugs, losing sleep, or sleeping in separate bedrooms.

In this case, however, I didn't fit into any of those categories. By morning, I was a frustrated walking zombie. When I sat down at the table for breakfast, the first sound I heard was Peter's voice. It reverberated in my ears as if I were in a heavy metal concert.

The effect of the ear plugs on my hearing over-night was astonishing. When I put my hands over my ears and told Peter what was happening, he lowered his voice to a softer tone. Fortunately, my ears returned to their normal hearing range within seconds. By then, laughter was the sound relieving all of us.

The next day, Jean drove downtown and came back with a box of nasal strips. I told her how much I appreciated her efforts.

According to television commercials, nothing was going to work short of an operation. That night, Jean snored louder than ever as the nasal strip dangled from her nose.

After all was said and done, there was an important, unexpected result from Jean's snoring. It happened when I spent the second night on the couch downstairs.

Since I brought a book with me, Janet saw the light on at two o'clock in the morning and came down the stairs to check it out.

If we didn't have the next three hours of girl-talk, I would have missed a great opportunity. It was the most meaningful conversation I ever had after meeting someone with whom I felt an instant kinship. Jean's snoring became a blessing in disguise and Janet was the rainbow after a storm.

Earlier in the day, Janet read some of my travel stories. As an avid reader of travel magazines, she encouraged me to think seriously about publishing them.

Janet had great conviction about setting me straight. "You're an explorer of life with a special ability to find humor, excitement and a connection with people," she explained.

My brain was still questioning her, *"Really?"*
Many of us are often blind about our talents. We need to see ourselves through the eyes of others until, hopefully, it finally becomes obvious.

I told Janet about wanting a passion that took me away without effort, just like other things which had held my interest. That's when I told her about my watercolor painting experience. After I made seven paintings and framed them all, I never had the desire to paint again. Surely if I were a gifted artist, I would have been driven to paint and pulled into it despite myself.

"But the pen is your paintbrush," she insisted. "You paint pictures with words."

Still questioning myself, I wondered if she could be right.

After all, I do find myself drawn to writing without effort. Late at night, thoughts come and I write them down. I've kept a diary all my life. English was my favorite subject. I published a news magazine and self-published two books. Why couldn't I see what Janet was telling me? Was I just too close to the forest to see the trees?

Finally, at four o'clock in the morning, I dared to believe Janet was correct about seeing me as an artist with a pen. She went upstairs an hour later to catch what little sleep was left.

When the early morning sun came through the living room window, feelings of relief and joy had come over me. I finally found my passion. How interesting. It was always there, right under my nose.

New Orleans, City of Extremes
2007

As my plane hovered over New Orleans, swamp lands stretched out as far as my eye could see. They appeared harmless from above until I reminded myself about the part they played in the long-suffering city of extremes.

The pot-holed streets, dilapidated buildings, fractured walls and up-rooted sidewalks were dispersed amid the hoopla of the New Orleans' jazz come-ons. Unfortunately, it had been that way for a long time, and definitely before Katrina ever came to town.

Despite the abolishment of slavery and segregation, the plight of black people still lived there. Along with the flood waters caused by an ill-conceived levee, her visit brought the city's inherent apathy to the surface as well.

It was obvious. The community had been robbed of its dignity from misdirected funds. Education of their youth had been dampened by corrupt government officials who stole twenty million dollars ear-marked for the school board.

Fortunately, efforts were being made to stop the run-away evil infesting the historical city. According to some people, the hard-working church people had been the ones putting their city back together when FEMA stepped in.

After speaking with my travel hosts, Frank and Diane, I felt their genuine interest in making my stay memorable. As she drove up to the airport curb, Diane waved me into her car and placed Mardi Gras beads over my head. Then she told me how wonderful it was to meet me. After she pulled into her driveway, I went onto the front porch where Diane's homemade sign welcomed me with my name on it.

That night, the three of us dined out in a local restaurant. Diane and Frank told me they wanted to show me the city's local spots as well as tourist areas.

The French influence was seen everywhere in the city's architecture, airport loudspeakers and street names. New Orleans' unique melting pot of French, German, Spanish and Sicilian cultures was a surprise to me.

Since I was drawn instinctively to the design of exquisite older homes, Frank drove past upper class neighborhoods. The houses lining the streets were so ornate they looked like huge white birthday cakes.

Despite everything I heard or read about the fun-filled, jazz-based city, nothing educated me about the goings-on along Bourbon Street. When my hosts drove through the French Quarter, I marveled at its French architecture. At night, however, the sleazy side of the French Quarter was brought into view.

Yes, I was ready for a lot of rowdy behavior, but I was surprised by the uninhibited women standing on bars, raising their shirts to show their bare midriffs. I had hoped it wouldn't be seen from the street and exposed to children and conservative people passing by.

Nor was I ready for the stream of *Hustler Magazine* girls displayed in large reprints along the walls of strip joints. At least the Las Vegas Strip hid such overt sleaze or relegated it to areas away from its finer spots.

Nine days before Mardi Gras, there were more than seven small parades. Most of them were attended by locals who came out despite the drizzling rain. I was touched by those who participated in the parades or dressed up in crisp uniforms to play in the band despite the cold, damp weather.

The floats weren't as large and detailed as those on Mardi Gras day, known as Fat Tuesday. Masked float riders threw beads to the crowds frivolously. Some were cast away in plastic bags containing multi-sized beads. By-standers filled little red wagons with beaded necklaces. Some float riders tossed them so high that they landed in trees, on telephone wires, or into the streets as useless discards.

Ironically, on the actual day of Mardi Gras, tourists would be clamoring for them around larger floats. They would be catching beaded necklaces while pushing each other to get just one.

Conversation in New Orleans was measured much like time before and after Jesus was born. However, in this case, it was neither B.C. nor A.D. My questions were answered with Before Katrina or After Katrina.

When inquiring about the population of New Orleans, the answer was, "Before Katrina, it was over 1.5 million and 70% were blacks. But after Katrina, it's about 1.2 million and now only 60% of the people are blacks."

It's been two years since Katrina was there. It has been hard for these people to forget about the devastation continuing to plague their beloved city. They embraced their history held so dear and talked about it frequently. Newspapers and television programs focused every day on the up-dated effects of Katrina. Discussing the subject was inescapable.

With tears in her eyes, Diane's emotions were heart-warming as she described how Katrina had brought neighbors together. Their southern hospitality stretched out to one another. They helped their homeless people who lived under freeway passes or in dome-shaped camping tents. It surely must have felt like an insurmountable task at times.

After I tasted the flavor of what made New Orleans famous, Diane shared what was in her heart about her beloved city. Diane's indomitable spirit was obvious.

"Sub-contractors ripped off other contractors. They took their money from the top and disappeared, leaving us holding the bag. So now there's no money to fix the roads and repair the buildings, and it's stifling hot and humid almost all year round. But we love to eat our great food, and we love to laugh, dance and enjoy our music. This is really a great place to visit and we have the only culture of its kind, although it's not a good place to live. But, no matter what, people don't leave New Orleans where roots run deep and strong."

That night, Diane filled my stomach with her great New Orleans cooking, Creole style. Scoops of rice with beans, okra and a tomato base left me licking my lips.

I told Diane how much I enjoyed her great cooking. Then I asked her about some real New Orleans dancing.

My words triggered Frank and Diane into taking me to a place where the locals danced. Diane prepared me for a treat of Rock n' Bowl where a Zydeco music fest was happening.

Feeling confused, I began questioning myself.

Did she say Rock n' Roll with a southern accent? No, she definitely said Rock n' Bowl.

As we headed for the local bowling alley, I tried to imagine such an incongruous set-up.

Reaching the top of the stairs, I saw over 100 people on a make-shift dance floor. They were right next to the bowling lanes filled with people knocking down pins.

The four-piece black band played its washboard beat for people from all walks of life. Those who were bowling, as if in two different worlds, were in a separate consciousness.

It was there in the real beauty of that unique culture where whites danced with blacks and everyone wore a face of joy and laughter. It was there where feet stomped so loud, the floor vibrations shook ten-foot high speakers. It was there, in that blissful moment of unexpected extremes, when I realized that was the reason I had to come to New Orleans.

We're all in the Same Boat
2007

Jean and I had booked an Alaskan cruise before we took our Canadian road trip. The ship would be setting sail three days after our return.

When she offered to stay home, I told Jean we were definitely going together on the cruise and would find a solution to her snoring. After all, with a little ingenuity, we could make it work.

We finally agreed to take sleeping shifts on chaise lounges in the ship's library. Since Jean didn't want any part of the nightlife, I was glad the early evening shift became mine.

Although we hadn't pre-registered online two days before the ship set sail, it actually worked in our favor. When we entered the boarding area, since most of the people followed the ship's request, they were standing in the Preferred Check-In line.

The regular check-in line was short. There were only four people ahead of us. Those in the Preferred Check-In line would be boarding long after us. From the look of things, I'd say we were definitely in the check-in line everyone preferred.

When the boarding procedure began, I noticed how things were different from my first cruise four years ago. After turning my luggage in for inspection, I found myself making several mental adjustments.

Following two body searches and additional checks on my hand luggage, I finally stood at the check-in counter to fill out more paperwork and show my passport.

The agent pointed a hairdryer-like contraption toward my face and took my picture. That photograph became my ticket to ride. It was also my room key and proper identification when leaving or returning to the ship in every port. Whenever it was passed through a computer system, my photo showed up on the screen, indicating that, yes indeed, I was definitely one of the good guys.

Bottom line, after extensive scrutiny, I was now cleared of terrorist suspicion. What an interesting thought while boarding a ship for a delightful cruise.

While walking up the ramp to come aboard, I was offered sanitizing gel by a crew member. All surfaces that were possible to clean had been disinfected before anyone set foot on the ship. Reminders about washing our hands were posted above sinks in all public and private bathrooms. Sanitizing gel dispensers stood in front of each buffet line.

Hopefully, with extensive anti-germ warfare in place, a virus epidemic would be prevented. World-wide coverage of past outbreaks informed people about these issues. Precautions became necessary to prevent passengers from suffering as well as an immediate halt in the cruise line industry.

My mind finally made its last adjustment. *Ah, the pleasures of taking a cruise still awaited me.*

After everyone came on board, television and loudspeaker announcements informed all the passengers about their required participation in lifeboat safety in case of a ship evacuation.

We had twenty minutes to find our cabins, put our life jackets on, head for the hallway, and find signs directing us to the outside decks. From there, we had to form groups based on matching numbers and letters inscribed on our life jackets.

The count-down had already started. I felt like a soldier called to attention for roll-call. If you've ever wondered how it felt to be 'just a number,' this was it. My number was 2648, the same number on my cabin door.

After crew members called out the first few numbers, people responded with the well-known phrase, "Here!" A minute later, deep in the somber crowd of more than 100 people, the next person yelled out, "Bingo!" Most of us found it hard to restrain ourselves from laughing.

It reminded me of those serious situations back in school when someone was deliberately saying something funny and we couldn't keep ourselves from cracking up.

When the lifeboat safety routine was over, we were asked to return to our cabins and remove our life jackets. By then, I was wondering if another precaution awaited us. *Was I actually finally going to be able to forget about the threats of terrorist attacks, viruses, and drowning?*

Frankly, if there were precautions about getting lost on the ship, I would have gladly welcomed them. It took me at least one day to become oriented about the decks of a ship that looked like an eight-layer cake.

Just when I understood where everything was located, another announcement stumped me. After arriving in our second port, instead of disembarking on the same deck on which we came aboard, we were instructed to leave on a tender located on Deck A.

Hearing that put me back into brain confusion. *How would I know about such a deck? My cabin was at the opposite end of the ship and I still hadn't found an elevator that went to Deck A. Now what's this about a tender?*

Later, I found out a tender was a small, motorized boat. It took people ashore when either the ship was too large or the water was too low to pull up to the dock.

By the end of the second day, I was still flagging down crew members for what seemed like an endless barrage of questions. Although there were maps about the ship in our cabin and near the elevators, it took me too much time to decipher them, and then to remember where they were directing me to go.

When it came right down to it, knowing where to go on the ship wasn't really my problem. It was how to get there depending on where I was standing at the time.

Actually, that just created more questions for my tired brain. *Let's see. Where exactly am I?*

First I had to figure out where the front end of the ship was facing. The day we left port, a band was playing at what I thought was the rear of the ship, only to find out the ship was backing out. My brain took a double-take on that one for a few seconds.

The front end of the ship is called 'forward.' Instead of calling the other end the 'back' of the ship, it is referred to it as 'the aft.' If they could just call them 'the front of the ship' and 'the back of the ship,' it would make it a whole lot easier for people like me.

Aside from that, there were always questions in my mind about where things were located. On what deck was the dining room? Where was the entrance to the third deck promenade? At what end of what deck was the buffet located?

Then there were places to find for onboard activities: the casino, dance lounges, the library, a computer room, outdoor and indoor pools, and the movie theater. How about the places to play trivia, listen to lectures, and do things that made the voyage enjoyable aside from eating our way to oblivion?

By the third day, I was finally able to find my way around except for locating bathrooms. They always seemed to be around the corner to the right, then to the left. Oops, that was the men's bathroom, an embarrassing place to walk into if men were using the urinals. After turning the next corner and to the left, there it was. Wrong again. It was another men's room. I went the extra feet to the ladies room wondering if the ship's designers were men.

Although assigned seating was only in the dining room, it didn't take long to figure out that I was better off eating at the buffet most of the time. Since the buffet was open until midnight, it had more food selections and we didn't have to wait for service.

Besides that, I didn't have to deal with the formality of the dining room. That's where everything depended on what was ordered as an appetizer, soup, salad, entree or dessert. One by one, each fork, spoon and knife was added or removed according to each course. It was like the changing of the guard in the silverware department. Everything was done with precision as the waiters flashed courteous grins to which I responded with appreciative smiles. That's a lot of work just to get something to eat.

When I ate in the dining room, no one passed on dessert. How could they? The extensive selections were brought to our table on display as if we still didn't have enough to eat. The most appealing part of the meal was paraded before our eyes, daring us to resist the urge to have two or three desserts.

However, we really weren't going to do that unless we were eating at the buffet. Why not eat like that in the dining room? Everyone at the table would look at you as if you were a glutton, that's why.

In my opinion, cruises were designed for two reasons: eating and spending money. Although there aren't any redeeming values in eating, it's entirely different when it comes to money.

During the first day at the gym, the instructor told me most people gained ten pounds during the cruise. So thank goodness for shopping. It also may have been the only activity people had if they didn't go to the gym, walk around the promenade deck, or go dancing at night.

It's actually healthy to spend money in the ship's boutiques, the sidewalk sales and stores in every port. Otherwise, much of the time would be spent on sight-seeing excursions which require sitting in buses, vans, horse-drawn buggies, and jeeps. So when it came down to it, shopping was really the best way to keep people on their feet.

Cruises were perfect for older folks and people who wanted to travel without hassles. They were happy with the trade-offs by seeing places for a few hours in each port. They didn't have to fly from here to there, find buses, take taxis, or drag their suitcases in and out of hotels.

When everything is said and done, how much do we really remember about things we saw in museums, art galleries, on guided tours, and everywhere else we wanted to experience? Maybe the highlights of cruises were what many of us needed.

After all, we didn't wind up with jet lag after sitting in cramped airline seats for what felt like endless hours. Come to think of it, people didn't need time to rest up after a cruise either. That's got to account for something.

On the other hand, if gaining weight were a serious issue, that's another story altogether. Cruises took up a lot of vacation time when it came to eating. For me, eating judiciously presented some real challenges. I was able to maintain until the last three days. Living in Las Vegas and eating in buffets had trained to walk past bread, potatoes, pasta and sweets. However, those desserts on board were hard to resist by the fourth day. By then I was on a roll.

Fortunately, I was still one of the few holdouts at the gym. When I went for my daily stretches the first few days, every machine was taken and the place was jam packed. Things had changed by the third day. The gym was practically empty.

The night before the cruise ended, I went to the midnight dessert extravaganza. At that point, things were put back into perspective for me after arriving when it was almost over. Two-thirds of the displays filled the length of the indoor pool on both sides. Most of the food had barely been touched. I wondered what was going to happen to all the uneaten food.

My mind jumped to thoughts of John, a man whom I met during lunch in the dining room a few days ago. He was sitting close to the window at a table with two other couples. John was quiet and didn't take part in the conversation. He looked out the window most of the time.

After I asked John what he did professionally, he said, "I'm the chaplain of Special Forces in Afghanistan." He was taking the cruise with his wife whom he hadn't seen for seven months. John's service required spending the last eighteen years apart from his wife with short vacations like this cruise.

Later that day, I saw John as we were going ashore on a tender. It gave me the chance to talk with him about what was really going on 'over there' and how his men handled everything. He verified the news we got through the media. But then he said it wasn't what really happened over there most of the time. It was actually worse.

Suddenly, I wondered if he didn't want to talk about business on his vacation. "Not at all," he assured me. "People don't usually want to talk with me when they find out about my job. It's too much of a mental burden for them."

John's haunting words stayed with me during the next three days. Unfortunately, although I never saw him again, I thought about what he faced each day in his work.

It reminded me of the World War II era when Hollywood made more musicals than any other time in history. People in the armed forces and loved ones at home needed to forget, even for a few hours, about the tough realities of life.

Cruises were designed to help us relax, leave stress behind, and explore the wonders of our world. Being happy was easy for some people. They found joy and laughter wherever they were. For them, a cruise ship was a large floating playground. For me, it was the people I met unexpectedly who made my travels special.

There was another man on the trip whose work took him away from loved ones for many months. His name was Jimmy. He sang and played piano in one of the lounges.

When Jimmy sang every night, he invited those around him to jump in and finish his words to popular songs. His sense of humor and "*Name That Tune*" games brought all of us closer together.

Jimmy definitely had a knack for being happy and enjoying every slice of life. I had a few chances to talk with him after closing time and between my sleeping shifts with Jean.

During our last night at sea, he talked with me about his life onboard. I especially enjoyed his story about a recent cruise in which the ship was privately booked by a group of nudists. Imagining people naked at the dining table, on the dance floor, and in the gym, I asked Jimmy how the crew handled the situation as the only people on board who were wearing clothes.

"Some crew members declined to work that cruise because of their religious beliefs," he said. I knew Jimmy must have handled it perfectly. With a well-defined impish grin, he said, "I concentrated on making a lot of eye contact!"

I would like to have seen John again, just to take him to the piano lounge for a generous slice of 'Jimmy Time.' Maybe he would have felt like the rest of us when we took musical strolls down memory lane. If John were there, Jimmy would have remembered his name. Then he would have cheered him on, hoping John's team would win one of Jimmy's funky prizes.

No matter where we were or what we were doing, it was always good to feel connected with people on the most basic level. On our last day at sea, I enjoyed watching people hugging others goodbye. Those were Kodak moments for me.

Jimmy gave us those every night. He made us comfortable about letting our hair down. Being encouraged to reach out to each other, we shared his music that stirred our souls.

Although there were almost two-thousand strangers on our ship, in those precious moments, the people who sang with Jimmy were all in the same boat.

Roundup at Round Top
2008

Joyce and I met through our travel club two years ago. She was a single woman who owned an antique store in San Diego. After my delightful three-night stay, we felt the beginnings of a new friendship and talked about taking a trip together.

Two months later, Joyce called with an invitation. "How would you like to come with me on an antique buying trip for my store? You can fly out of Las Vegas and meet me at the Austin Airport. After you told me that you were on the *"The Antiques Roadshow,"* I knew you had a good eye. C'mon, we'll have a great time and you can help me find some interesting pieces."

When the famous show came to Las Vegas, I was invited to appear with my mint-condition, metal-bound wooden chest. It took three people to lift it when the professional movers brought it to the show. While on the air, two Sotheby's representatives told me the history of my 1880's rare find. I had paid $100 for it thirty years ago. They assured me it was now worth $15,000, thank you very much!

Although I had never been to an antiques fair, the thought of hanging out with Joyce was going to be a wonderful experience. Hoping to help her find a few unusual antiques added to my excitement about being there.

Both of us arrived at the Austin Airport close to the same time. After lunch, we headed for Round Top. As we came into town, we stopped at its only traffic light. The main part of Round Top was one block long and less than a block in two other directions.

My attention was drawn to the surrounding green fields and prairie lands which were breathtaking at that time of year. Spring flowers were in profusion. They were dominated by bluebonnets, the state flower promoted by Lady Bird Johnson.

When we spotted more than fifty homes, I wondered why the road signs claimed only seventy-seven people lived there. As it turned out, Round Top was the closest hill country to Houston and Austin which were an hour's drive away. Since those were vacation homes, their owners weren't considered residents of Round Top.

That tiny patch of central Texas countryside also became an attraction for perhaps the most unusual antiques fair in the world. Although small events went on throughout the year, every spring and fall their largest shows drew over 30,000 antique dealers and 50,000 buyers. Most of them assembled under tents to do business.

Along with laid-back southern folks and city slickers, we were there for a show of that magnitude. Everyone was committed to a search through Round Top and its four neighboring towns. The challenge was in finding what Joyce wanted while searching amid a constant flow of buyers and sellers.

She found out about the fair two weeks before it started. Joyce said it might be difficult to find somewhere to stay. The only places available were thirty miles away. She had already reserved a room in a questionable motel. It came with a warning to bring pillows and sheets. Bottom line, bugs might be joining us.

There was, however, an outside chance that we might have a place in Round Top at the eleventh hour. A week before we arrived, Joyce contacted a local real estate agent who said a rental might come through. That's what happened after we arrived.

We followed the agent's car along a dirt road and turned into a driveway the length of a football field. When I saw cows grazing along several acres of pasture land, it reminded me of my childhood on a dairy farm.

As we drove up to the large house, the owners were waiting for us on the front porch. When they welcomed us in, we entered through the main hallway. It was decked out in a dark green wainscoting and flowered wallpaper. Long wood planks had been perfectly laid along the entire hallway floor.

The owners offered information about their 110-year old German-style home. They said the house originally had two large bedrooms. Over the years, three other rooms and an attic were added. Children withstood severe weather changes in the attic during the winter and summer months.

Many 100-year old framed photographs adorned the hallway and bedroom walls. They revealed stories about the lives of people who lived there at that time.

In my bedroom, a framed naturalization certificate displayed a photograph of a Czechoslovakian woman who sat erect as if she were proud to have become an American.

Several *"National Geographic"* magazines were on my nightstand. They were published in 1943. It raised my curiosity about reading a magazine published a year after I was born.

While thumbing through a few editions, I noticed a barrage of advertisements focused on World War II. On one page, Bell Telephone Company expressed their "devotion to winning the war." In the middle of the next page, GM Diesel Power informed readers about the war traffic doubling the volume of freight. Bell and Howell referred to "your peaceful home movies that will have to wait." Westinghouse Generators wanted to "make power for a nation at war." Sidebars encouraged people to "Keep America Strong and Buy More Bonds."

Thoughts came to mind about how we would feel if we were at war today. Back then, solid support was obvious for what was happening overseas. Reading those stories made me realize people felt like they were all in that war together and were willing to do their share.

Admiring their strength, I saw a common thread with the people who had lived in the house at that time. In their photo-stories and hand-written notes, I saw more than what met my eye. Those people were humble and grateful for their simple lives, which made those hard times easier to bear.

After the real estate agent left and Joyce cleared the car of her luggage, she was ready to begin her search at the Marburger Show where someone said we would be seeing the finest antiques. It was estimated that there were over fifty listed shows and locations, each housing hundreds of vendors.

When we arrived, I entered the nearest tent to the parking lot. Gazing into booths on either side of the aisle, I saw rows of exquisite antique furniture which were beautifully displayed with decorator lighting.

Occasionally a design magazine drew my attention. When I saw the pages on which particular antique pieces were being featured, I appreciated their fine level of sophistication.

There was only one difference between looking at them in a magazine and seeing them at the antique show. At the show, they were on display in a cow pasture. They were poised with dignity on such items as roofing shingles, plastic tarps, wood shavings, or freshly scattered hay.

Many vendors rented space in buildings with less expensive booths. The most expensive ones cost twice as much with a $1,500 fee. Those antique dealers figured it was worth the price. They knew air-conditioners in those buildings were an enticement to buyers who wanted to stay indoors a lot longer in the hot, humid weather. Besides that, they would be able to use the only public toilets available.

Porta-Potties were provided in the tented areas. That fact alone kept me from drinking my usual large intake of water every day.

Joyce wandered past each booth trying to find what she came to buy. After taking a second look, she stopped and talked with dealers about the history, condition, and price of the items she considered purchasing. The choices seemed endless between furniture, clothing, jewelry, silverware, quilts, cowhides, paintings, sculptures, and anything else that was woven, carved or welded.

Since she only had a few days to look for them, Joyce hoped to round up what she wanted to buy. Fortunately, she bought several items the day we arrived, snapping them up without question. When I saw a few smaller items that Joyce might be interested in, she grabbed them up immediately.

Several items actually raised my eyebrows. I couldn't imagine buying a display of what looked like skeletal remains of large insects and centipedes. They were displayed under glass, sitting upright and supported on metal rods. All of them were tagged with a wholesale price in the hundreds.

A nearby chair made me stop in my tracks. Designed with an upholstered cowhide seat, it sat on four hairy legs, hoofs and all. No one could have paid me to sit on it. I got the willies just looking at it.

Transporting Joyce's purchases across the United States was a major factor. Although she had planned to carry small, fragile items on the plane, larger antiques required shipping arrangements. Joyce had contacted a reputable dealer who owned a store in San Diego and was renting a booth at the fair.

Like most dealers, he transported his goods by truck to and from antique shows. He agreed to pick up Joyce's items and charge her less than a trucking company. More importantly, he wouldn't lose, dent or break her things, nor would he leave them on the side of the road. Unfortunately, that wasn't an unusual occurrence in that business.

After three long days of antique-hunting, Joyce closed in on places we didn't have time to explore until then. It was early morning. We still had a few hours to search through tents along roadsides near the major shows. It only took Joyce a few minutes to see that most of them were junk by her standards.

We had enough time to stop where a dealer suggested looking for antiques more suited to her taste. He was right. They were housed in flimsy, open metal structures along the side of the road. Despite complete exhaustion, Joyce was thrilled to see many eclectic things.

The temperature dropped to 45 degrees and a thunderstorm warning alerted us to possible rain. Texans say, "If you wait a few minutes, the weather will change."

The wind was also kicking up. Dust suddenly flew everywhere. It tangled in my hair and forced my eyes shut as I walked from one outdoor area to another.

It was our fourth and last day of the show. Joyce retraced her steps to locate what she had decided to buy. She looked at her list and talked about where to go first and in what order the antiques would be picked up. The man with the truck arranged to pick up her purchases in two different locations.

Suddenly the wind came up with great force. It howled through tent openings and caused canopies to flap wildly. I got out of the car and sank into the mud where a 30-minute downpour got the best of my shoes. In my mind, I apologized to the car rental people who would be spending a fair amount of time getting the caked mud off the carpet.

Fortunately, the rain subsided to an occasional drizzle. As Joyce's antique furniture was wrapped in plastic, the only fight left was in battling the cold wind. She stood by as she watched her new treasures lifted carefully into the truck.

It wasn't until that moment when I understood the intense journey antiques could take before they wound up in the hands of their next owners.

People like Joyce drag themselves from tent to tent, fighting winds and rain while plodding through the mud. Their newest acquisitions travel through several states before they are finally displayed in pristine condition. I could never again look at antiques without that realization.

The Twilight Zone
2008

Originally, Mimmo had agreed to a two-week home exchange. However, in his last email, he offered a different arrangement for my stay in his east coast Italian home. He also reminded me that Vico del Gargano was the favorite place Italians went for their vacations.

He wrote, "I am offering you a week for $50 a day. It is a reasonable price for a vacation there."

Mimmo also wrote about the town's pure Italian culture. He said it would be of no interest to typical American tourists since no one spoke English there. That meant I would be challenged to speak Italian all the time.

Since Spanish and Italian languages had many similarities, and I could speak some of each, I accepted Mimmo's offer. After staying for a week in his home, my plans were to head north for another visit with Emilio. Since my last visit, he left Milan and moved to the countryside with his sister, Dina, to take care of their elderly mother.

This year's trip began in Sorrento, a magnificent town sitting along Italy's southwest coast. The scenery was breathtaking. Houses hung on cliffs overlooking the sea hundreds of feet below. After spending three days in a Sorrento hilltop hotel overlooking the incredible Amalfi Coast, a part of me was reluctant to leave.

The next morning, I waved an imaginary magic wand, wishing I could return to my hilltop paradise. Then, I grabbed my bags, stepped into the hotel's mini-van, and headed for the train station.

Just thinking about the four-hour haul wore me out. The first segment began in the Sorrento train station where I had to purchase a ticket for the one-hour ride to the Naples train station. From there, I had to purchase a train ticket to Foggia. Three hours later, the train would pull into its station where Mimmo promised to be waiting for me.

The trip was exhausting and harrowing. At one point, I had to run down a long tunnel with other scurrying passengers so we wouldn't miss the train. Unfortunately, I came to a dead stop after spotting an escalator ahead. Taking a deep breath, I forced myself onto its moving stairs.

Going down an escalator was scary for me, especially with a duffle bag on wheels and an over-sized shoulder bag. While I was working in a New York City department store as a teenager, I had a frightening experience.

When I stepped onto a moving escalator heading down, the high-heel shoe on my left foot got caught in one of the narrow metal slots on the escalator steps. Envisioning myself being pulled under the disappearing steps, my brain prepared me for being chopped into tiny pieces.

It wasn't until the last few steps when I told myself to bend down, pull off my shoe, and yank it out of the metal slot. I managed to get off the escalator just before the stairs disappeared under the floor. I haven't been the same since.

People tell me I am courageous to be traveling alone. I'm not afraid at all. For me, without question, it's approaching an escalator going down.

My next train connection was the one-hour ride before arriving in Foggia. That gave me time to re-group for the next segment where I would have to scramble to change trains in the middle of nowhere.

When the train pulled into the station, it wasn't easy to read the Italian signs about the next train to Foggia. At that point, I only knew the train was going to leave on a different track.

That meant I had to go down a flight of stairs, through a tunnel, up another flight of stairs, and onto a platform with a choice of two tracks. I thought about what to do before the train arrived so it wouldn't leave me behind.

Then it hit me. *My train ticket! Yes, that was my way out!*

Noticing an old woman standing nearby, I showed her my ticket. Thankfully, she knew what was needed and flagged down a young man. When he agreed to take my bags to the correct train track, I began running behind him like an insecure chick chasing frantically after its mother.

When the train arrived in Foggia, I spotted Mimmo through the window as the train pulled into the station. He had described himself on his website as "an athletic, sporty 41-year old with graying hair." It was easy to recognize him standing on the platform among simply-dressed folks.

Mimmo wore large sunglasses, sandals, blue plaid Bermuda shorts and a white cotton Polo shirt. His collar stood at full attention around his elongated neck. I wondered if his shirt had been starched with a secret ingredient to keep it in place no matter how he turned his head.

While walking to his car, Mimmo asked about my journey but made no offer to pull my suitcase or carry my bag. That's when I reminded myself about his internet comment requesting I bring a light suitcase.

By then, I thought it was simply a warning about being on my own from the start, light suitcase or not. At that point, I figured Mimmo was not about to do anything that would definitely bring his collar down.

After an hour of pleasant talk in his car, he stopped and pointed to the town ahead. As we entered Vico del Gargano, I saw a village of earthy agricultural residents. We passed a small park where men were gathered on benches. Mimmo said they spent their time relaxing there at the end of their workday.

Heading up a narrow cobblestone passageway, we entered a medieval section where remains of a castle towered over ancient buildings. As we passed scaffolding and construction sites, he said those once-abandoned buildings were being renovated. Mothers and their children were sitting outside on cement steps. Their dogs were close by without collars or leashes.

While turning a corner and squeezing as best he could into an impossible space, Mimmo said we couldn't go by car any further. After handing me the luggage, he walked ahead assuming that I would follow.

Around another corner, I faced three inclines daring me to pull my suitcase to the top. At that point, I asked myself an important question. *How long can I endure this obstacle course?*

Three turns later, we were there. As I looked up to see the front door, it looked like the photograph on his website. But that's all it was, just the door, not a two-story house with two bedrooms. It was actually an old apartment building.

After he reached the top of the stairs, Mimmo unlocked the door and told me about two other keys. By then, I was talking to myself. *Two other keys? For what?*

Entering a small foyer, Mimmo pointed to a bedroom and a bathroom. Then, two more steps up and to the right, I saw a room with a tiny table and two chairs. Assuming this was the dining area, I asked where the kitchen and living room were located.

That's when I found out about the second key. Mimmo unlocked a door which led us outside onto a small, wrought-iron balcony. He suggested I spend my mornings dining outside.

I still had another question swimming around in my brain. *Well, that's dandy, but where's the kitchen?*

As Mimmo started walking up a set of steep stairs, he beckoned me to follow. At the top, he used the third key to open the final door. The kitchen, dining and living room were all packed into a narrow room.

The second bedroom was just above my head, perched over the living room on a piece of 8' x 8' fiberboard fastened with metal brackets. After thinking about sleeping up there, I noticed the flimsy ladder. Realizing the second bathroom was also four steps down from the kitchen, I decided the first floor level was my best bet and I'd eat out.

Bidding me farewell, Mimmo gave me the keys and his cell phone number. Although there wasn't a phone in the apartment, he said there were public phones three blocks away.

The next day, I discovered three things about those phones. They didn't take coins, they didn't accept calling cards, and they couldn't reach Mimmo's cell phone.

The worst was yet to come. It began with the ringing of a loud church bell in the building next to Mimmo's apartment. It rang on the hour as well as every fifteen minutes.

It wasn't until midnight when I would come to know it more intimately. It was after the children stopped yelling and the dogs stopped barking when I realized the bell would ring every fifteen minutes, 24 hours a day.

After two sleepless nights, staying through the week-end was out of the question. *What was I talking about? There was no way I could make it past another day!*

Now determined to leave, I told myself there had to be a way out of my misery. I decided to walk into the village and take a look around.

As I walked through the maze of old buildings, I finally saw what was ahead. It looked like a ghost town except for men sitting on those benches.

When I reached the bus-stop, nothing was there. I searched for the place where bus tickets were sold. Since it was only two o'clock, nothing was available for another hour.

Suddenly, I had an overwhelming sensation of being in Rod Serling's television series, *"The Twilight Zone."* Streets were deserted, communication was gone, and the few stores were closed. The only option I had was the half-mile trek back to my dungeon of bell-ringing torture.

Vowing to return an hour later, I turned to my sense of logic and came up with my next plan. While standing outside a bank, I would wait for a young man to exit. In the last ten years, students were learning English in Italy. If I got lucky and waited for a man in his early-twenties, he would be my best choice. Since he probably had an account there, my chances were better in selecting someone who wouldn't rob me.

Hopefully, he would tell me where to find the ticket office and the bus to the Foggia train station. Better yet, if he knew someone who could help me, I would gladly pay that person to drive me back to Foggia.

Three minutes after standing in front of the bank, I approached a clean-cut young man leaving the bank who appeared to be twenty-five years old. Antonio spoke English very well. After explaining my situation, I asked him for information.

He didn't know anyone who could drive me to Foggia. Although he couldn't help me, Antonio suggested I take the bus. That's when I told him about my luggage problem. Bottom line, I still faced carrying my luggage downhill in the severe heat along the half-mile walk from Mimmo's place.

Then he asked if I had to leave right away. "If you meet me here at three o'clock," he said, "I will come with my car and drive you to the train station in Foggia."

I couldn't believe my ears! Was I really going to be plucked out of this nightmare and set free? As Antonio was leaving, I promised to meet him there on time.

At 3:05 PM, Antonio drove up in his car with his pregnant wife in the backseat. His wife spoke no English and was content to sit back and relax. After I got into his car and pointed the way to Mimmo's apartment, Antonio explained his situation.

"I own a sporting goods store which is closed at three o'clock. Then I open the store again at five o'clock. That's why I can drive you to Foggia now."

Much like Mexico's siesta time, most Italian businesses close from noon to five o'clock. This was the time-slot that dear, 30-year old man devoted to helping a lady in distress.

After refusing to accept any money, he drove through the ancient maze and retrieved my luggage. Then we were finally off to the Foggia train station.

Feeling overwhelmed and grateful, I told him he was most welcome to spend a week's vacation with his family in my Las Vegas home. At that point, if it were possible to give him the world on a silver platter, I would have done that, too.

Bidding farewell in Foggia and waving goodbye to Antonio's wife, I headed into the train station. Anticipating the long trek back to Naples, and then the train to Sorrento, my hopes were high in returning to my hilltop hotel paradise again.

Since it was getting late, it was best to call ahead and let the owners know about my return. While I waited on the train platform, a young man sitting on a bench was kind in offering his cell phone for my call to Sorrento.

When someone answered the phone at the hotel, I was told there were no rooms available. Gianni, one of the family owners, suggested I walk to other hotels near the Sorrento train station since they usually had rooms available.

I walked into the first hotel and asked for a room. No luck. A conference in town took up all the rooms for the next week.

The desk clerk offered me the phone to call my hilltop paradise again. This time, I spoke to brother Dino. By then, it was midnight. If worse came to worse, I was prepared to sleep on one of the chaise lounges on the hotel roof-top.

Thankfully, Dino took pity on me. He told me to walk to the pick-up location in town where his brother would fetch me in the hotel mini-bus. They decided to move me from room to room as people checked out over the next few days.

Sighing with relief, I quickly headed for the meeting place in town. That's when it all sunk in.

I was really returning to my Sorrento hilltop paradise. Who said magic wands don't work?

Dina and Emilio
2008

After taking the train north from Sorrento, I met Emilio in the Milan train station. Seeing him again made my day.

We arrived at the country house an hour later. His sister Dina and their mother were waiting for us. I was eager to see "Mama" again, especially after learning more Italian. It was important that I could speak with her easier during this visit. She was a warm, happy woman who always gave me long, loving hugs.

Unfortunately, the trip was over-shadowed by the sudden global economic collapse. Italy was Europe's most bankrupt country. It had also been riddled with corruption for many years.

To make things worse, fingers were pointed toward the United States as the obvious culprit in the stock market crash. Italians were being fed information through newspapers and television with updated reports twice a day.

My three-week stay with Emilio and Dina became more meaningful as we talked openly about their concerns. They looked at their immediate future as a halt in their budgets. Pondering their fate, they focused on the television screen for hours, voicing their fears of what was ahead.

At one point, Emilio became emotionally aroused. "We were sold rubbish! The Americans sold bonds to foreign banks with nothing to back them up. Predictions were made over the last twenty years that this was coming as there are no surprises here by people who have been paying attention."

A few days later, I was surprised when Dina told me about Italy's dependence on America. She said, "Yes, we listen to your music, we watch your television shows, and we watch over 75% of your movies."

During the next week, Dina told me about America's continued presence in Italy and the rest of Europe over the years. She began by asking, "Why do you think Europeans don't like Americans today?"

Without hesitation, she explained further. "We forget that they saved France and Italy. Europeans think Americans want to take over the world. They expect everyone to have a democracy which is unrealistic and doesn't always work, not even for us."

Dina believed we were in Iraq for its oil. "After all, why would Americans spend so much money for democracy unless you are positioning yourselves? When the Middle East attacks Israel, you will have enough allies in Iraq. We have seen America as the richest country in the world until now as it faces economic collapse. It will affect all of us. We have been living in a country deep in debt and on credit which was doomed to fail. Now we are paying the price."

Listening to Dina made me feel very grateful. We were friends who could express ourselves easily without discomfort or threats to our friendship.

One day, Dina talked about her past during World War II. "During Mussolini's Fascist regime in the late 1930's, Enrico Fermi, a member of our family, discovered the radiation needed to create the first atomic bomb."

"We were all allies in World War II, until Mussolini joined forces with Hitler. Fortunately, since Italy had ninety percent of the world's monuments, it was agreed that monuments and old churches would not be bombed."

"As a young girl, I lived in our country home here in the small village of San Pietro where we were born. I can still remember the sounds of bombs exploding. Thanks to a miracle, I was saved because a nine-year old girl was killed in our nearby field when they were dropping the bomb."

"My grandmother thought it was safe in her house when Emilio and I napped upstairs one afternoon. Usually alarms warned of approaching danger, but suddenly a bomb exploded in the field near her house. It was carried by the wind into the bedroom where it smashed windows and sprayed me with glass."

Dina recalled a sad memory about her mother. "She was crying from seeing dead German soldiers in the courtyard, especially one who was still alive and suffering. My mother was afraid to help him because she might be shot by American soldiers. The Americans were there to kill the Germans who were there to kill the Italians who were against Mussolini. Italians could be killed in the crossfire at the very least."

"I remember the day American soldiers came through the door of our home. I was afraid they might kill me because we did not know who could be trusted. My father hid until he was sure Americans came in the house searching for Germans. When he knew it was finally safe, he made scrambled eggs for the American soldiers. They gave my parents their chocolate and bread which was scarce at that time."

From that day on, I had a better understanding about the life Dina had lived as a child. Her life changed as an adult when she became a caretaker. After her husband was diagnosed with cancer and required constant attention at home, Dina took care of him until he died in 2004.

Two years later, her 92-year old mother could no longer live alone in the 400-year old country house in San Pietro. Dina knew it was impossible to take care of her mother's needs if she lived in Milan. When she and Emilio discussed the situation, they both gave up their busy lives in Milan and moved to San Pietro.

Since Dina's return to life in the country, things had changed drastically in San Pietro. "Now couples are having one or two children in our country of zero population growth," she said. "So making ends meet is a serious issue. Over 80% of the people living here are old. The few students who still live here want to move to large towns or big cities when they are older."

Emilio adjusted well to living in the country again. As a 72-year old bachelor and a retired language professor, he devoted most of his time to writing historical and political novels. His books were written in his sanctuary, a 1,500 square-foot room which was the original hay loft. The view from up there hadn't changed. It still overlooked 200 acres of fertile land.

The area below Emilio's living space used to be the barn. After its renovation 25 years ago, it became a huge family room with massive doorways connecting the room to the original, up-dated house. Between the two attached buildings, Dina had plenty of room for her shabby chic Milan furnishings in their now 4,000 square-foot country home.

Her day started at five o'clock in the morning. Dina's chores began in the kitchen. She baked apple strudel or fruit cakes for breakfast. They looked and tasted like they came from a bakery.

"If I were younger," said Dina wistfully, "I would have come to America and opened a restaurant. I know it definitely would have been a success."

Dina's passion for cooking was obvious. Every meal could have competed with the finest restaurant. She served lunch at one o'clock in the afternoon as the biggest meal of the day. Everyone took a nap after lunch. Then Dina served dinner at seven o'clock in the evening.

She also enjoyed being the head of the household. Aside from cooking, Dina's days were filled with cleaning, laundry, ironing, gardening, and grocery shopping. Despite all of her daily chores, she never complained.

Although her days were busy, Dina still preferred her life at home. She was relieved knowing she was no longer entangled in the inequality between men and women in Milan's working world.

During those difficult years, she took care of all household chores while working full-time as the Fleet Manager for an American car rental office. Dina worked there for 35 years without a raise.

Her job had been replaced by a man who received three times her salary. He then hired two other people to do her duties. Since Dina performed the jobs of three people, she was offered twice her salary if she trained the new employees during her last two months in the office.

After moving to the countryside, Emilio enjoyed driving to Milan regularly to meet with his colleagues, former students, and friends. He was a stimulating conversationalist with a witty sense of humor. His intellectual side was satisfied when he could share his knowledge of Italian history, art, and religion.

Emilio was also fastidious about the way he dressed for the city. He always wore a conservative suit with a long-sleeved white shirt. If he had dinner plans, he wore a tie. In warm weather, Emilio removed his suit jacket, rolled up his sleeves, folded his jacket carefully and carried it over his arm.

Although Dina and Emilio enjoyed their busy lives in Milan for almost forty years, they were happy living a quiet life in the country. As children who grew up with the horrors of war, they had solid values.

I felt honored to be friends with two such strong people who were dedicated to their mother. They cared for her until 2015, when Mama was 105 years old and passed away peacefully.

Endurance
2008

Alligators were thriving in Charleston, South Carolina. They lurked on the banks of lagoons and along golf courses. According to my cousin Richie, if one started chasing you, it was necessary to do one important thing. You have to zigzag. He further explained that although alligators were fast, they were not able to shift directions easily. That meant you had to zigzag if you hoped to out run them.

Richie and his wife Lily lived close to the beach and a golf course. He told me about the day his golf ball landed near an alligator's tail.

"Actually he was sleeping," he explained. "Alligators only come out of the water to warm their bodies in the sun. If an alligator opened his eyes even the slightest, you can be sure, I would definitely be zigzagging!"

His story reminded me of those who lived in other parts of the country. People who lived on the west coast thought it was worth living there despite the earthquakes, fires and mudslides. Then there were those living in the north east who endured hot, humid summers and freezing winters. People living in the mid-west had to put up with tornadoes and hurricanes. To me, the people who deserved a medal endured roaches, ants, mosquitoes and alligators on a daily basis. Those people lived in Charleston.

When it came down to it, all of us had pros and cons about where we chose to live. Some of us never moved because of deep family roots. I moved to Las Vegas thinking my endurance level would be minimal. There weren't severe weather extremes except in the summer. It was better, however, than dripping wet from extreme humidity, being attacked by bugs, and trudging through deep snow.

Years ago, Charleston had a serious flooding problem. Since Hurricane Hugo destroyed trees and homes, regulations were changed in the flood zones. New homes had to be constructed ten feet above the ground. Most were esthetically camouflaged by trees, bushes and lattice.

The cicadas took me by surprise during my walk back from the beach one day. As I came around a corner, an ear-piercing noise erupted from the bushes. It sounded like thousands of insects getting zapped simultaneously by electrical impulses.

Nothing was there when I stopped and turned to see them. Suddenly the noise stopped, as if on a dime, and then it started again seconds later. Baffled and covering my ears, I walked away as fast as I possibly could.

After telling Richie what happened, he said, "They were cicadas. They look like winged beetles with grasshopper legs and bulging eyes. But there's nothing to worry about. You won't see any. They just make that awful, deafening noise."

Their house had other issues inside. "No matter how much bug spray we use," said Richie, "the ants and beetles as large as roaches come into the house. We have to be careful about not leaving any food on the counter and to put our cereals away in plastic containers."

Avoiding the bites of outdoor critters reminded me of what I had read recently. It was suggested that I hang a fabric softener sheet on the outside of my pants or shirt before stepping outside. To my amazement, it worked.

Then I performed a second test by leaving my legs exposed. A few minutes after rubbing my arms with the fabric softener sheet, my legs were heavily bitten and my arms were totally free of invasion. This was great news for my cousin who could finally get rid of his bug spray.

Regardless of the nasty pests in Charleston, I could certainly understand why people lived there. It was a visual paradise, a joy to walk on the beaches, and its 1800's architecture was eye candy.

As an art lover, attending Charleston's "First-Friday-of-the-Month Art Walk" was a highlight. Many art galleries offered hors d'oeuvres and wine. Others displayed art outdoors in quaint gardens where people could sit on benches to look at them.

On the following day, a visit to Drayton Hall made an impact on me. The grounds represented an undisturbed historic account of plantation life. It was the only unrestored plantation in Charleston.

Drayton Hall had survived the American Revolution and the Civil War despite hurricanes, floods and modern times. Its bare-bones look gave me a true, unaltered image of the racial issues and sacrifices made. My thoughts turned to the slaves who had lived and worked there.

Only one building remained as a reminder of their rudimentary life. Looking in the window of the privy, I was surprised to see an outhouse for five people. It had five holes cut into one slab of wood. Thinking about people without freedom was one adjustment, but knowing they had no privacy on the most basic level was another.

Hardships were endured and there was certainly no escape from the hot, humid summers and insect bites. I kept imagining them dripping in sweat and covered with sores.

I was moved again by nearby hallowed ground tucked in the shade along the river. That solemn place under the trees honored the slaves who lived and toiled there. Slightly raised and rounded, the plot of ground was encircled with rectangular concrete slabs, all nameless.

Looking at that place of honor left me feeling envious. As far as I knew, there were no traces of honor in my family heritage.

It was verified when Richie and I looked at his family photographs that night. Honoring our family's heritage had little importance to me, but it hit home that day. There was little history with my grandparents whom I rarely saw as a young girl.

Richie adored my father but had no photos of him. "I'll make copies from my own collection when I get home," I assured him.

That was especially important. After my parents divorced, my father moved into his sister's home when Richie was a young boy. At that time, my father became Richie's best friend and mentor. Interestingly, his mother became mine when I was an adult. We reminisced about his mother as he shared the photographs he had of her.

Pulling out another picture, he looked at it with a soft smile. It was a photograph of Richie's grandfather on his father's side. He said it was the only one he had of any grandparent.

There was something special about that photograph. Richie's grandfather was born in 1874. He was in his twenties when the photograph was taken. It was in perfect condition with beautifully embossed edges.

"Richie," I said with excitement, "this is a great photograph to frame! It's also a statement about a place and time in history that speaks of your heritage." He held the photograph high in his hand and looked at it more closely.

"Yes, I agree! This is wonderful!" he exclaimed. "I will definitely do that." Then he put the photograph on the table, separating it from the rest.

Later that night, while recalling the history of those who endured slavery and discrimination on the Drayton Hall plantation, my thoughts turned to Richie's grandfather. He had lived in Europe and suffered discrimination, just like each Jewish generation before and after him who experienced those injustices.

After returning home, I began looking through the photograph collection given to me by Richie's mother before she passed away. Thumbing through them, I wondered why my aunt kept one of her father. He was a tyrant who had beaten her and my father. As frightened teenagers, they eventually left home.

Many abused children who endured physical and emotional pain, still need to hold onto memories that would hopefully bring them peace. In my aunt's photograph of her father, he was smiling.

No matter how awful my grandfather was, I needed to remember the hard life he also endured and that he was part of our family heritage. Otherwise, Richie and I wouldn't be here.

The Last Time
2008

Thoughts about the visit with my cousin, Richie, returned over and over again after I came home from Charleston. My focus was entirely about my father. When my diaries came to mind, I looked through them for what I had written about in our last visit together.

In 1980, I was 38 years old, raising two teenage boys alone and couldn't afford to fly across the country. Fortunately, I borrowed money from a friend so that I could visit with my father in Louisiana.

*****

June 7th - Lying in front of the fire last night, I was overcome by a strong urge to see my father. I felt like he was calling me, not literally, just a feeling that I should see him soon. Maybe I could go before the play gets under way. I'd have to see my father within two weeks.

June 17th - I think of my father and my emotions explode. I wonder if I can handle my visit with him. I don't want to go away with a lot of sadness. I can't stand losing him now. Why am I doing this? Is he really calling me? I don't believe it now. I wish I did. It's too late.

June 18th - I'm pacing down now after an emotional bout with thoughts of seeing my father. I think again about not having him in my life. I never knew the everyday adoration of a father because he lived so far away and couldn't afford to visit. I hear myself inside yelling, *"Why couldn't it happen for me?"* My father would have been so great. I can remember a few special times on the farm. They were simple and wonderful.

I hear how much my cousin Richie loved him, how close they were when my father lived with them after my parents' divorce. Through him, I've come to know more about what a special, loving and creative man my father was.

I talk of my father as if he were gone already. I feel as if I'm going to a funeral only he isn't dead yet. He might as well be. He won't even know I'm there. If ever I wanted to believe in a power beyond, it would be now, having to see my father for the last time. I can't bear to see him if I'm going to walk away in sadness.

I think only of his days in total absence of the world and himself...sitting...staring...just sitting and staring...and that's all. Why does his body bother working anymore? The world goes on and by. Now I have a mental image. In a few days, I'll have a visual one.

I can't accept not having my father all my life. I imagine living it out now, alone with him for a few hours for the first time in almost 25 years, holding his hand, leaning on him, telling him what I feel, talking about those special, simple times....and then, hopefully, letting go.

June 19th - I told my friend Sharon about my depression, or whatever this state is that's overwhelming me. We spent hours talking about metaphysical aspects of life. "If you believe your father will know you," she said, "he will." Now I finally feel ready to see him.

June 20th - Emotions are running high now. It's hard to hold back tears. Hugging David goodbye, I whispered, "I love you," in his ear.

"I love you, too, Mom."

Chris is taking me to the airport. As he drove up, I turned to David, "Thank you so much, son, for taking care of everything while I'm gone."

At the Airport:

Donna knew how much I needed a camera. Just before I had to board the plane, she pushed her way through the airport to lend me hers. She knew how important it was to take pictures of my father.

And now I'm alone, up-tight about flying as usual. I walked outside to the plane as it sat waiting for me. "I'm coming, Dad. I'm almost there. I'm coming."

In Flight:

There are so many people on board. I'm feeling alone but content being apart from them. I pulled out my script from the play while searching for my diary. My mind is easing as I see the familiar reminders of home.

We will be landing in two hours. When I read this, my trip will be over. I felt so much peace, so much eagerness to see my father all morning. I looked out the window through take-off and wasn't afraid at all, seeing the wing flaps open and watching us rise up.

I thumbed through Lauren Bacall's book, catching her passages about Bogart's death and I became emotional. I went into the bathroom and saw myself in the mirror, trying to keep the tears back. "Okay, let them out," I told myself. "It's alright. It's going to be alright. You're going to be strong. Come on now, you're strong." Finally I believed it. I was fine again and ready to go back to my seat. I feel okay again, all my pieces intact, solemn but not sad, quiet but not afraid.

I feel definite about dealing with my father's wife, Myra. I need to look at her calmly and tell her how I feel and what I want. She need not be afraid of me as a threat. I must assure her of that.

I must have that special time with my father, not letting her chatter, her endless chatter, get in my way. I imagine holding my father's hand through it all, even if she parades her children and grandchildren through. I must be with him. It will be the most whole day of our lives together.

June 21st - I can't understand where my mind is taking me. I hope this writing will keep me together. I drift a lot, wanting to get away. I can't stand Myra rattling on and on. She doesn't know what I'm feeling. I tried to tell her about my needs but she won't hear me. I go into the bathroom just to be alone.

She won't let me be with my father. I've asked for one hour, just one. I asked again. She finally agreed to go shopping tomorrow. She's so scared of me and what I might do here.

She talks incessantly. I don't answer her. I don't start the conversation. She talks about everything and anything, in detail, like someone gone mad.

Maybe that's why my father is senile. Maybe he just tuned out, like he used to when he had enough of the farm but he couldn't get away.

And now he sits in his chair or goes to his bed, back to his chair, back to bed and she gives him directions when it's time to eat or bathe. I want to hold onto my special moments with my father. I don't want this to be happening.

Before I saw my dad come out of his bedroom yesterday, Myra told me he never recognizes anyone. She didn't want me to be disappointed when he treated me like a stranger.

But when he saw me, he knew who I was. I went over to him and we cried.

He kept saying, "It's unbelievable. It's incredible," as he kissed me over and over, sobbing, then laughing and sobbing again. "Thank you," he said over and over again. My father kissed me more in those moments than I could remember in my whole life. My tears kept coming, as they still do. I can't get past them.

June 22nd
In Flight: Going Home

I'm finally alone and onboard. Myra left me with Dad for an hour. First we went into the living room. While I sat on the floor holding his hands, we smiled at each other. Then he took my hands and I watched him rub them gently, like he did when my feet were cold and he rubbed them until they would get warm.

When I asked him about the farm, he said, "That was a long time ago." I was amazed he remembered that part of his life. When he didn't recall anything thing else, I stopped asking questions.

After ten minutes, he went to bed and I followed him. It felt natural to lie down next to him. I always did that when I was frightened in the middle of the night.

Now he was holding me tight, playing with my nose and cheeks. He held my hand and rubbed it with his, gently, continuously, and lovingly. He kissed my eyes just like he used to. He straightened my clothes and held me close, looking down at me all the time.

Then he stroked my head the way he did when I was a little girl. I felt safe and calm under his loving touch and I always fell asleep. It was the same even now. I fell asleep in his arms.

I woke up when Myra returned and came into the bedroom. Her first words were surprising. "Do you want to go home with your daughter?"

Had she forgotten that he doesn't understand anything? Seeing us together had led her to believe we knew something she didn't. She felt threatened. I told her my father was staying. She had nothing to worry about. I wasn't taking him away from her.

When it was time to leave, I kept thinking of the minutes left and that I'd never see him again. Then he got up and went back to bed. I followed him and said goodbye while the lights were out.

Touching his face for the last time, I couldn't hold back the tears. He cried, too, knowing it was the end. After telling him goodbye and how much I loved him, Myra came and took me away.

The ride to the airport seemed endless. Myra made sure her whole family met me. I hardly said hello and the car was full of people and their chatter.

I sat back and closed my eyes. I didn't care who anyone was. It was easy tuning out after a minute or so. My headache and my dad were all I felt.

The airplane is pulling out to the runway now. Red and blue lights are ahead.

Off I go. Goodbye, Daddy.

Paradise Found
2012

When I was 33 years old, I moved to Ashland, Oregon where I bought a 100-year old fixer-upper. A few months after moving in, I told a neighbor my house needed a face lift. He kindly referred me to his friend, Chris, a school teacher who had become a professional carpenter over the years.

Chris and I worked well together. He could read my mind as I described the designs for my house's renovation. One afternoon, his girlfriend Kate came by with lunch. None of us knew then that it was the beginning of a forty-year friendship.

Back then, Chris and Kate were pot-smoking hippies living on a shoe-string and making music together. Kate and her seven-year old son, Andy, lived with Chris in his Ashland home. He had a large organic garden behind the house and an out-building where he made guitars in his spare time.

Kate was pregnant the day we met. Three months after their daughter Willow was born, Kate said, "You're not going to believe this. I'm pregnant again. We decided that if it's a boy, we're going to name him Chance."

Several months after Chance was born, Kate made the same announcement. "I'm pregnant again. If it's another boy, we're going to name him Bo." During that pregnancy, Andy was diagnosed with a malignant brain tumor. He died two months after Bo was born.

Kate's life went on auto-pilot. She struggled with the loss of her son, Andy, while breast-feeding two babies, keeping house and maintaining a consistent flow of ripening vegetables. Although they had been recently married, Kate fought desperate yearnings to run away. By then, she was afraid of having a nervous break-down. But she didn't.

Kate turned to the teachings of Jehovah and found solace there. After she chose to become a Jehovah's Witness, Chris followed close behind. For the first time since they met, Chris cut back his long hair and shaved off his beard.

Nine months after Bo was born, Kate said it again, "You're not going to believe this. I'm pregnant." If it were a boy, they would name him Amos. Her depression deepened with the prospect of having three children under the age of four. She worried about not being able to handle things.

Whenever Kate lost her temper, she wasn't able to forgive herself. She couldn't appreciate all the times she smiled at her children sweetly, kissing their toes and making them laugh with funny cartoon voices. Unfortunately, Kate never felt like a mother who was good enough.

That was also around the time the 70's recession swept through the valley. Chris was hard-pressed to make ends meet as a carpenter whose work was seasonal. He renewed his credentials and returned to teaching.

When he was offered a job on the Oregon coast, they bought a house near the ocean with enough acreage to build a cottage for rental income, a greenhouse, and enormous organic gardens.

Chris always had the patience of a saint. He was more laid-back than Kate who fought for more organization while maintaining a constant flow of vegetables, fruit, eggs, and children.

Their focus had never changed. They were still free spirits, angels really, who were extraordinarily devoted to raising their children well.

They prayed over each meal and gave thanks. Neither television nor outside resources were used for their entertainment. They were content visiting friends, enjoying nature and making music. Their children danced, sang and played music right along with them.

One morning, I was there an hour before their Sunday morning service in the Kingdom Hall. During their family gathering in the living room, Chris spoke about two Biblical stories and what they meant. Then he asked the children what they would do if someone treated them badly.

Without hesitation, and in the tender words of young children, they explained their sense of compassion and forgiveness. I remember that moment well, feeling like a fly on the wall in the Walton's house.

There were times, however, when I had wondered if a family such as the Walton's had ever existed. *Could people really be that nice to each other and love their neighbors?*

I had come from a divorced home and my own two marriages ended poorly. While raising my sons alone, often with little or no support, I had yearned for what Chris and Kate were able to accomplish.

The proof was there as their children grew into young adults. Each one stayed in the fold and married another Jehovah's Witness. All the children, except Chance, lived in a nearby town, no more than an hour or two away. The entire family came together a few times a year when Chance and his wife flew in from upstate New York. Then there were all the in-between times when the siblings went camping, fishing or river rafting.

In my last visit, I stayed with Willow for a few days. She was a 28-year old mother of an infant son. Watching Willow diaper her sweet boy brought back memories of when I used to diaper her. *Wasn't it just yesterday when she was four years old and I took her to watch ballet in the park? How long has it been since I watched Willow dance with her brothers in their living room?*

Now Willow sings and plays guitar with her parents at local cafes and county fairs. They call themselves, *"Homemade Jam."*

After my visit with Willow, I stayed with Chris and Kate for several days. They always talked openly when I was alone with each of them. I knew what was in their hearts, on their minds, and that they spoke the truth. They shared their most difficult times with me and how they found contentment in being together despite their different personalities.

Some people wondered how I could have such a friendship with Chris and Kate. After all, they lived in a different world and spoke a different language. Their home was a place where every nook and cranny was filled with religious books, magazines and their Bible.

Fortunately, the language of love has no boundaries and judgments. What binds us has always been the love and respect we have for each other.

The last night of my visit was on a clear July evening. The sky poured moonlight on their front porch as I settled in on a cushioned swing. I enjoyed the fish pond to my right, the gardens on my left, and the chickens scratching for feed.

A few minutes later, I heard Chris and Kate singing as they were coming back from an evening walk. Their sweet voices were still floating in the air.

When they came up onto the porch, Chris picked up his guitar and started playing as he sat down next to me. After Kate lit several candles on the porch, she sat beside Chris and played her concertina as they sang in harmony. When my voice joined theirs, I became overwhelmed with joy.

Looking at Chris, I smiled and said, "I'm in heaven."

Then, smiling back at me, Chris said softly, "Well, this isn't Heaven, but it certainly is Paradise."

After thinking about his words, I said, "Yes, this is definitely a heavenly moment in Paradise."

When Rivers Run Deep
2012

David wanted to give me a special present for my 70th birthday. "Whatever you want, Mom, just let me know," he said. I was thrilled about receiving a generous gift from my precious son.

When I told my friend, Carol, she suggested taking a river cruise through Bavaria, Austria, and Holland. Although she knew I didn't care for large cruises, she said river cruises were different.

"There will probably be less than 150 people on the ship which pulls into a different port every day," she said. When I agreed to go, she booked the trip quickly knowing we would be leaving in two weeks.

A few days later, I looked at the detailed itinerary for the first time. During the 14-day trip, we were going to be in Germany for twelve days.

Thoughts of Uta flooded my brain. I recalled the years she was a German baroness and her father worked for Hitler. Then I reminded myself again about how German people felt when they learned about the concentration camps. Her father carried shame and guilt for the rest of his life and instilled it in his children. These were innocent people who loved their country and felt stained forever.

Two years ago, I met a woman who left Germany after she couldn't rid herself of guilt and shame. She said there were many others like herself who had felt the same way and had done the very same thing.

After reading more about the cruise itinerary, I became very uncomfortable. The trip also included our visit to the Nuremberg courtroom where Nazis had been sentenced to death for their inhumanities to man.

My brain raced with disturbing thoughts. *How could anything positive come from discussing the execution of six million Jews?"*

We were going to see a country noted for its story-book beauty. I couldn't imagine bridging that gap while cruising down the Rhine, Mein and Danube rivers.

After flying into Vienna, we boarded our small ship with 120 passengers onboard. As we passed magnificent Bavarian scenery, it was a continuous feast for my eyes from the dining room, lounge and sun deck. Over the next few days, guided tours through charming Bavarian towns were an added delight.

A few days later, after having lunch onboard, we left the ship for another guided tour. As our tour bus headed for Nuremburg, it stopped at one of Hitler's huge arenas which had been built for him to rally 5,000 people at once.

Hitler was clever when it came to widespread propaganda. He produced, *"The Peoples' Radio"* to reach every German home. The Volkswagen was designed to give proof to his promise of economic growth.

When the bus took us to the Nuremburg courthouse, I thought about the other Jewish people on the tour. For most people, this was a history lesson. Personally, it was more than I ever wanted to know. By then, I was wondering how many Jewish people were having the same mental struggle as mine. Were they asking themselves the same question? *What is the purpose of dragging all of this up again?*

Suddenly, hearing the familiar sound of Nazi police sirens in the streets, I got the chills. It was a frightening reminder about their search for Jews during World War II.

As we entered the famous courtroom, I sat down reluctantly, wishing I hadn't left the ship. The narrator began talking as soon as all of us were seated.

Although most of our tour guides had been Europeans, the Nuremburg narrator was a charismatic American. He spoke like a lawyer addressing a jury that needed to know the importance of its history there.

Until that moment, I didn't know that event had set a precedent for future trials of atrocious crimes against humanity. The United States, England, France and Russia led the way for international cohesion. Those trials defended and supported new laws to protect the world from future tragedies.

For the first time in my life, I viewed the events of the Holocaust as the sacrifice of six million Jews whose deaths were no longer in vain. That thought made me sit up straighter and feel proud to be there.

Now I listened ardently to details about how that courtroom was different in 1945. Pointing to the windows, the speaker said, "They were covered to prevent possible sniper attacks. The wall behind you had been taken out and a balcony was put in for spectators. The new wall was extended even further back for reporters and photographers."

Pointing to the chandeliers, he said, "They replaced the harsh, bright ceiling lights. That's why you often saw those on trial wearing sunglasses. They sat in the two front rows. Helmeted guards stood against the wall behind them."

It became apparent at that moment, and every day thereafter, that everything was being done on the tours to show respect for Jewish people and to honor the passing of Holocaust victims.

After we left the courtroom, all of us were escorted to a main plaza where we had an hour to wander around. Spotting the courtroom narrator, I asked him about the responses of Jewish people who experienced this tour. "Some come away without relief," he replied, "but most feel an inner emotional freedom."

I told him about Uta and the shame her people felt. He told me Germans took pride in their country until Hitler came on the scene.

"Many young people lost their fathers in World War II. Needing a father figure, they looked to Hitler for one. Germany was suffering economically, people were out of work, and Hitler told a great story about how he would help them. Here was an Austrian with a small-man mentality and no previous political experience. Like most politicians, he promised a future of abundance to a burdened people. Unfortunately, they were the younger generation whose gullible idealism made them easy prey for Hitler's tactics."

Later that night, another man gave a talk onboard about how Hitler came to power and used the Jews as scapegoats. "Christians weren't allowed to lend money for profit," he said. "So Jews were looked upon unfavorably for their money-lending practices despite their influence in making Germany prosper and succeed."

The next day my emotions were high as we were guided through places where Jewish memorials stood out and a band played a Jewish folk song in a German restaurant. A rabbi spoke about 106,000 Jews who lived in Germany despite high security in his own synagogue and the vandalism in many Jewish cemeteries.

By now, I was very impressed. My hat was off to Grand Circle Tours for their back-door approach in winning over Jewish people like myself.

After returning home, I called Uta about what I learned on my trip through Germany. She was pleased and reflective, reminding me again about the importance of that historical time.

"Your understanding of the Hitler situation will hopefully also help your Jewish friends to let go of the hate and horror they still feel toward the Germans. I have many close Jewish friends. None are holding any of these terrible things Hitler did. It was a very dark history we will always have to accept. And, yes, we should never forget and must make sure it never happens again."

Original Aboriginals
2013

Native Australians are known as Aboriginals, or Aborigines. They are much like our Native American Indians. Both continue to keep their cultures separate yet integrated in today's world.

Aboriginals were invaded generations ago by alcohol and sexual diseases. They no longer lived as healthy and long. Men died around fifty years of age. Women survived until they were in their mid-sixties.

Some Aboriginals had made life transitions. They were in touch with positive aspects of technology while still maintaining harmony with nature.

Several days before our tour of Sydney, Australia, we headed to New Zealand. Emily, our cruise tour guide, took our small group to Cairns where she talked about her experience as a resident there.

Emily spoke about the difficulties Aboriginals had in today's world. There was a negative tone in her voice as she talked about the trouble they were causing and why people resented them.

After we arrived, everyone got off the bus and turned their attention to throwing a boomerang and a spear with the assistance of Aboriginal men. Then, as an introduction to their culture, we were entertained by male and female performers who danced, sang and played native instruments.

Thrown in the mix were small gatherings with Aboriginal men who told us about the ways animals were hunted with various handmade tools. Some were designed to stop larger animals while others caught smaller creatures walking low on the ground.

When we were broken up into small groups, Smoke, a very friendly Aboriginal, was the narrator in my group. He answered questions about his part in the integrated life in which he was paid to perform. He no longer shared everyday life in his village, visiting his people only four times a year.

After the session was over, I managed to have some private time with Smoke, asking him why he chose this life and being away from his family. After deciding to make the transition, he brought one of his wives, his 12-year old son and three daughters with him.

"I want my children to be educated like me. We need to bring what we learn back to our people," he explained.

By then, I was confused. Originally, he said his people didn't need the other life offered in towns and cities.

"My people don't need money or things. We hunt for our food or grow what we eat, and we treat one another equally. We don't need jails because our laws are strict and punishments are painful. Our people heal slowly, so they have time to think about what they did wrong."

"If they don't return to our laws, they become cast out forever without ways to defend themselves against danger and survival in the bush. We do not fight with other tribes. All of us are peaceful and choose marriage partners for each other. We have our own medicines made from trees and plants, so we don't need hospitals and doctors. We respect and take care of our elders who provide us with wisdom."

"Those of us who choose this new path want others to move forward in their thinking and forget the past and the mistakes made between us. It is most important that we are the link to tie us together in peace and understanding, knowing that there is good in both cultures."

Our tour guide brought us to Sydney three days later. Like Cairns, Sydney residents had great respect by not littering anywhere. The city also provided free swimming pools and exercise equipment along the promenade areas.

After we arrived, I used my free time to visit The Art Museum of New South Wales where there were no admission fees. There were also no roped barriers to keep people from getting as close as possible to the objects on display.

My focus in the art museum was in locating Aboriginal art. After asking where they were, I spent almost an hour studying Aboriginal wood sculptures as well as bark and oil paintings.

Turning a corner, I spotted a docent giving an American couple information and decided to listen in. The docent was an older fascinating gentleman in his late seventies or early eighties.

When the couple moved on, I asked the docent if he could spend a few minutes with me regarding my confusion over what was going on with the Aboriginals.

He was more than accommodating about answering my questions and grateful for the opportunity to express his true feelings.

My probing questions also revealed my disturbing confusion. "Why do people have such judgment, criticism, and lack of acceptance when it's obvious that the Aboriginals' way of living is more in tune with life as it was meant to be on our planet?"

I continued with more curiosity. "Look at what our world has become ever since the Industrial Revolution. Yes, we have managed to land on the moon, but we are also unable to live in peace with the threat of being annihilated by nuclear power. It seems like we have progressed toward oblivion. The younger generation focuses on the need for superficial stimuli which only creates great stress. What happened to the simplicity of life which brings us peace?"

The docent gave my questions great thought. Then he showed me a very large painting of a man which had been created by an Aboriginal painter.

He was passionate about what he had to say. "Most Aboriginals today speak out politically about the different ways they have been treated," he said.

"Take this painting, for instance. Look closely at it now. Do you see how the man is dressed? He appears to be a pirate but without a beard. Look at his one eye. There is a patch over it to emphasize what he is. Now ask yourself why he is dressed like that. The painter is saying that a form of piracy invaded them."

Then, directing my attention to another part of the painting, he pointed and said, "Note at the bottom of the painting that there is a box with a head of an Aboriginal man in it. The painter is making reference to the beheadings of many Aboriginals whose heads were given to those who made experiments on them."

The docent took me to look at another art form, a sculpture of sorts. It had several rows of bats hanging upside down from a square-shaped, yellow, plastic clothesline.

"I don't know why there are only ninety-nine flying foxes (that's what bats are called in Australia), but notice how they are hanging on a square-shaped clothesline with a strange look on their faces. The clothesline is made of material which Australians use, but not the Aboriginals. In this sculpture, the Aborigines people are represented by those flying foxes. They hang there with looks of bewilderment, as if feeling out of place in that environment."

Finally seeing his point and what the artist was saying, I was fascinated and the docent knew it.

"Let me tell you now that I have been among the Aborigines people for many years," he said. "They are a wonderful people, no doubt. There are those who were born with a curious nature and the intelligence to explore and learn, like people of every culture.

If they reach for their potential, they will rise to a level of education and awareness that most people do not."

"These are the Aboriginals I have known and worked with. As they have integrated, they have also become aware of the problems in both cultures. It is most unfortunate, indeed, that man has been misplaced within himself. So as he struggles together and separately, he continues to find no place of inner comfort. It is, however, also interesting that the people like Aboriginals who faced oppression, are the ones who found more true answers about our purpose in life."

My mind became quiet until understanding filled its space. I finally understood why the Aboriginals weren't obstructed with a clouded view of life and why they were able to see its truth.

I shook the docent's hand and thanked him for his honest answers to my probing questions. I was grateful to have been in the right place at the right time to receive invaluable wisdom about the Aboriginal culture.

The Traveling Curve
2013

After Joan and I met at a dinner party, we decided to take an autumn foliage trip through New England. We always had a lot to talk about, especially since her knowledge of the business world was extensive. I also liked her quick-witted sense of humor and adventurous nature. Since Joan was a balance of focus and flexibility, I thought we had a pretty good chance of getting along.

Over the years, the famous phrase, "You get to know someone when you travel together," has always been true for me, especially when things went wrong. When that happened, staying calm and finding a solution was the key.

Joan and I made plans to be in the great outdoors while driving through five states. Stopping for art galleries, antique stores and on-the-spot sales were a given. Although Joan wanted to spend a lot of time at the seashore, my main focus was on seeing autumn leaves wherever they were. We actually went to twenty-four cities and towns in eight days.

At the beginning of our trip in Hartford, Connecticut, Joan said she preferred to drive, making me the designated navigator. I had no problem with that. Frankly, it gave me more time to look at the autumn scenery.

I told Joan about my restrictions. I couldn't read maps easily and became queasy trying to read them in a car going around curves. Left with a choice of Map Quest printouts or my GPS, she chose the GPS.

Although Joan and I shared similar interests, we expressed ourselves differently which showed up while we were paying for our rental car.

"Whoever drives has the choice of music and temperature controls," Joan informed me.

My mind wasn't ready to say something yet. *That's why she wanted to drive! Aside from being logical, she's manipulative.*

There was really only one answer, and only one way to put it. Now with a big grin, I said. "If that's the way it's going to be, I'll drive."

She explained her situation further. "That's how it was when I used to travel with my husband. But I also admit to being a control freak who wants my own way."

That's when I suggested doing things differently by creating a win-win situation.

And so we did.

Each of us shared the driving. We agreed to compatible temperatures and talked so much we never played any music.

She teased me about how much more I talked than she did. "As far as how much I talk, yes, I do talk quite a bit, but when I'm not talking, you're right there picking up the slack," I responded with a smile.

Joan also believed she was right most of the time. Although I accepted her beliefs, at one point, my sense of logic came on.

"So let me see if I understand this. If you're always right, that makes me wrong all the time. Well, I think I'm just as smart as you, so that doesn't make sense." Now I was teasing her and she knew it.

By the fifth day, Joan was annoyed when my GPS stopped getting satellite signals. After her patience ran out, she turned it toward me with a less-than-pleasant tone.

That's also when she told me people nicknamed her, "Miss Snappy Lips." We laughed about how well it fit her. I always appreciated people who knew their short comings and weren't afraid to admit them.

"Then if you get nasty," I said with a teasing grin, "I'll say, uh oh, Miss Snappy Lips is back."

And so I did.

The first time it happened, we were driving to a house in the countryside where travel club members agreed to be our hosts for two nights. We arrived after dark. When I say dark, that means the kind of dark where street lights didn't exist and you couldn't see house numbers which were posted somewhere else anyway.

Our hosts instructed me to look for the fifth house on the left. However, although my GPS was announcing our arrival, there was still a discrepancy about which of the two houses on our left was the fifth house.

I got out of the car and rang the doorbell of the first house on our left. The woman who opened the door didn't look like she was expecting anyone. After apologizing for my intrusion, she then graciously pointed toward the house next door. While going back to the car, I suggested Joan turn around in front of the garage where she had parked.

"It won't be easy," she said. Then she started driving backwards out of the driveway despite its severe curve. Joan ran over the grass three times and left deep tire marks in the turf. I finally got out of the car and directed her into the street.

By then, I hoped the neighbor wasn't watching us, or at the very least, she couldn't see the new design in her grass. Bottom line, we didn't want her to tattle on us to the people next door.

At the end of the next day, we drove back to our travel club hosts in the dark. When Joan turned onto the correct street, I recognized the correct house and turned off the GPS.

Joan was upset. "Why did you disconnect the GPS? Now we can't find the house, you Dip-Shit."

Figuring she was just anxious about backing out of the wrong driveway again, nevertheless, I had a different focus.

"Uh, oh" I said. "It looks like Miss Snappy Lips is back. And look at this! She's a name-caller on top of that!"

I told her no one had ever called me names. It was actually amusing at that point. We laughed uncontrollably in the dark.

Joan's great sense of humor was quite endearing. She claimed it also kept us from killing each other.

Assuring her it was more than that, I smiled and said, "It's actually my patience in putting up with you."

She admitted to having fights and getting over them. "But that's not my style," I said. "I don't fight. I'll be kind to you no matter how nasty you are. Then, if we can't work things out, I'll walk away. I know you want control, but I hope by now you know having your own way won't work for me. I prefer to negotiate what we want, choose what's important to each of us, and then take turns if that becomes necessary."

She said she wasn't used to doing it that way, but she was still willing to see its benefits. I sensed she wanted to get along as much as I did, at least until the trip was over.

"I know your first thought is about yourself because you were born that way. I accept that without criticizing or judging you. But I was born to be a team-player who wants both of us to be happy. To me, it feels like the best way to get along." Joan was listening.

"I have an idea. For the rest of the day, within every hour, try asking me in your very sweetest voice if there's something you can do for me." Although she smiled with amusement, she also agreed to try it.

By the third hour, she had it down pat. "You know," I said with a huge smile, "You're really getting good at this, Joan. You're even beginning to sound sincere!"

All kidding aside, my hat was off to her. "That's one big Brownie point for you," I said earnestly. "That's not easy for most people to do. Defenses go up and settling differences go down." Joan 'heard' me. That was another one of her great attributes.

We spent our last two days with our Connecticut travel hosts where hints of color finally surfaced. During the first day, we stopped at a yoga center before going through the woods on a scenic 33-mile drive known as Jacob's Ladder. When we arrived at the center, a beautiful lake and surrounding woods stood before us.

"I would love to stay for an hour!" I exclaimed. Miss Snappy Lips was adamant about staying for no more than thirty minutes and that was that. Since our interests differed, we went our own way, agreeing to meet in the parking lot.

Leaving me with little time to do much, I headed for the yoga center to find a thank you gift for our travel hosts. I found the perfect gift after looking around for almost twenty minutes. Then I went to the ladies room. Two minutes later, my cell phone rang.

"I need ten more minutes," Joan said blatantly with a sharp tone in her voice. She had walked down to the lake without realizing it was further than she thought. Now she needed more time to walk back.

After I agreed to ten more minutes, she hung up. By then I had just enough time for a short stroll along a creek.

When we met back at the car, I was quiet. Joan wasn't used to that. "Are you ok?" she asked.

"No, I'm not," I answered. "Something is wrong, but I don't know what it is. I have to work on myself to find out. I'm upset about you and that it happened while we were here, but I don't know when it started and why I got upset."

It was quiet for a few more minutes as I rewound the tape in my head about conversations we had earlier. When the answer came, I gave it to Joan.

"When you called to tell me you wanted ten more minutes, I wasn't upset because you wanted extra time. But you didn't ask if I was happy with that, or if I wanted more time for myself."

When she wondered why I didn't ask for more time if I wanted it, I told her Miss Snappy Lips was on the other end of the phone. She had already turned me down after we arrived and when I wanted more time to enjoy the autumn leaves. If she didn't want to share that part of our autumn trip, she could have stayed in the car or read a book, like I did when she walked on the beach without time limits.

"Bottom line, I felt hurt when you didn't think of me. But that's precisely where I went wrong. I expected you to consider my needs because you did that so well yesterday. What really happened is that you were being human and slipped. But I slipped, too. I lost sight of how long it takes for someone to 'get it.' My expectations set me up for disappointment. I forgot about accepting you the way you were. That's when I knew I needed to work on myself. The only person I can hope to change is me."

Joan listened quietly as I finished my explanation. "That's why I needed a few quiet minutes to do that. Now I'm free of frustration and ready to enjoy the rest of the day. Whew, I'm glad that's over! So, are you going to drive while I stick my head out the window and inhale this incredible autumn fragrance?"

And so she did.

We spent the next two days walking around a lake, wandering through meadows and looking at waterfalls. Rain threatened but it didn't come. Thankfully, I was able to go out and take more photos of the deeper autumn tones.

When we got back to the house before dark, drops of rain started and then stopped. Joan said she was going to pack up and put everything in the car. She was concerned about the possibility of dealing with pouring rain when we had to leave for the airport the next day.

After Joan put her luggage in the car, she went up the old wooden stairs in the back of the house and into the kitchen. A few minutes later, I decided to pack as well.

Years ago, I developed a system to avoid carrying heavy suitcases on short trips. I left my large suitcase in the car after removing things I needed for the next day. By packing those items into a small suitcase, it was easier to pull, lift, and climb stairs.

After Joan went into the house, I left the car keys on the seat knowing I would be coming down the stairs with my arms full. While pushing the remote, the side door would open, and I'd put my clothes on the seat. Packing everything in both suitcases would be the easy part.

Since my leg had been bothering me, I didn't want to climb the old wooden stairs more than once. When I got to the top and came into the kitchen, Joan was still there.

"I see that you left the car door open on your side," she said as she went upstairs to her bedroom.

Joan insisted on keeping the car doors locked at all times. In this case, we were parked in the back of a house on four acres, away from potential intrusion, so I assumed locking the car didn't really matter.

I gathered my things quickly with even more items than I remembered bringing upstairs. Clothes dangled from my legs and I could barely see the old wooden steps. By then, I was concerned about falling down the entire flight of stairs.

In the time it took to get my clothes, it started to rain, which made everything wet. After managing to stay upright on the stairs, I came down and went around to the side of the car.

The door was closed and the car was locked. I couldn't call out to Joan about unlocking the car since the windows in the house were shut.

Looking at the stairs, I faced the fact that I had to go back up to the house. By then, aggravation and frustration were building inside me. Some clothes threatened to fall out of my arms while others wound themselves around my legs. I went up the old stairs again, one step at a time to protect my aching knee.

After managing to open the door latch with my elbow, I called out to Joan. No answer. I called her name two more times in a louder, more audible tone.

When she finally replied, I called out for her to unlock the car. She was able to do that from the window of her room.

Once again, I went outside and down the wet stairs with my clothes. When I opened the car door and saw an empty space on the back seat, a sigh of relief came over me. After putting my clothes on the seat, I began packing my large suitcase.

Within a few minutes, Joan was standing beside me. In a sweet voice, she asked, "Is there anything I can do to help you?"

She also explained that she had closed the side door because it was starting to rain. "But I didn't lock the door," she said. "Maybe it locked by itself after a few minutes."

Nothing mattered by then. Joan was looking at me with kindness in her face. I replied, "What I need right now is for us to hug each other."

And so we did.

Life in a Fish Bowl
2014

During my European river cruise in 2012, I met two delightful couples. After telling them how much I loved Lake Como, they decided to join me in a vacation there this year.

Menaggio was the only Italian town on the lake with a large, flat plaza. It also had no cobblestone steps requiring people to climb steep hills. Some of my favorite times were spent taking walks on the flower-lined promenade extending along the edge of the lake.

While looking on the internet, I found a villa in the heart of town through the rental office of Holiday Homes. At the price of $80 a day, each of us felt lucky to be living in an exquisite villa for three weeks.

After we landed in Milan's Malpensa Airport, our chartered bus was waiting to take us through the magnificent Italian Alps to Menaggio. I purposely took the front seat on the right side of the bus. That way, I would have an unobstructed view of the stunning scenery below.

The bus slowed down as it entered the village of Laglio. Our driver reminded me of the tour guides in Beverly Hills who drove passengers past houses of famous Hollywood stars.

Calling our attention to the view directly below, our driver said, "Look down there. George Clooney's villa is right on the edge of the lake."

The three-story cream-colored building was unlike most villas. There were no ornate windows or walls in striking colors of peach, rose or terra cotta.

When we arrived in Menaggio a few minutes later, our driver parked in front of our villa gates. The mustard-colored, 150-year old building was surrounded by lush gardens. From its covered patio, I had a view of Bellagio directly across the lake.

The owners of the villa stood on the steps and welcomed us in. They had prepared a four-course dinner knowing we would be hungry and weary from traveling.

The dining room shared a spacious area with its ornate living room. From there, a long hallway led to the large kitchen with a casual dining area in the middle of the room.

Before serving dinner, the owners took us through the upper part of the villa. We were led into a large entry hall where we had the choice of a spiral staircase or an elevator to the second floor.

After taking the elevator, I saw four bedrooms with balconies over-looking the lake. There was a large bathroom at the end of the hall. When we were downstairs, I remembered seeing a second one near the kitchen.

All of us spent the next day exploring Menaggio. In the afternoon, I went to the Holiday Homes rental office and asked about the 26-mile boat tours along the lake. The two receptionists, Viviana and Manuela, also suggested taking the red train tour to Saint Tropez, the famous ski resort in Switzerland.

A few days later, George Clooney announced his intentions of marrying his fiancé, Amal Alamuddin, on the twelfth of September. However, he didn't say exactly **where** he would tie the knot. The mystery heightened when he said it might take place in Villa Oleandra, his favorite of the two villas he owned on the lake.

An immediate gossip frenzy spread throughout Italy about other locations the wedding might take place. Tour company operators, ferry boat agents and shop owners were more than willing to offer inside information about George's secret place. My friends enjoyed getting in on the fun by telling everyone they were expecting their wedding invitations any day now.

All of us boarded a boat for a tour along the lake the next day. After leaving the Menaggio harbor, we passed two small towns before the tour narrator began pointing to places of interest. George Clooney's villa was at the top of her list.

She talked about the stir of gossip George created about his wedding. "Mr. Clooney became the treasure of Laglio when the mayor made him an honorary citizen."

Clooney made several movies along the lake. When he drew more attention to himself, the town's real estate increased ten-fold, business boomed, and Laglio became world-famous.

After the boat tour, I stopped in at the rental office to ask Viviana's opinion about where Clooney might have his wedding.

"I think he will be married in his eighteenth century Villa Oleandra," she said. "At the very least, the wedding could take place in Villa D'Este where he dines often."

A minute later, she thought about another possibility. "Mr. Clooney might have the wedding on the island of Isola Comacina. If you take a different Lake Como tour, the boat will stop at the island for an hour."

She added more interesting information about the unusual place. "A large restaurant is on top of the mountain. You can have lunch there with a beautiful view of the lake below. It would be a quiet place for the wedding and very close to Mr. Clooney's village where he has a large yard with a private pool. He can also provide his guests comfortably in his 22-room villa nearby."

Then Manuela told me about the issues that George's friends had when they were recently married. "They warned him about problems with the paparazzi," she explained.

Dealing with the paparazzi was nothing new to George. He faced them wherever he went. There were times, however, when he wanted his privacy.

George bought his ten-million dollar villa in Laglio for that reason. The village only had one restaurant and one food market for its population of 960 people.

Mr. Clooney thought it was too small to be a tourist area and that it couldn't be invaded by fans and paparazzi. It wasn't an easy place for tourists to reach. The village was unavailable for bus and ferry routes and it was only accessible on small boats.

Heeding his friends' warning, Clooney decided to protect his privacy for the wedding. He approached the mayor about applying for the right to keep people from trespassing.

The law went in his favor. People were forbidden to enter his grounds. The mooring areas were also restricted. Boats had to stay 100 meters from his shoreline. Otherwise, boat owners and operators received a fine.

George took matters in his own hands. He installed an egg-throwing machine in his garden. It hurled raw eggs at boats coming too close.

Mr. Clooney was among other rich and famous people who were drawn to Lake Como. It had been a retreat since ancient Roman times. Winston Churchill and the Duke and Duchess of Windsor headed the list of world leaders. Mark Twain wrote about the lake in his first book. Paul McCartney and Elton John bought vacation homes there. And the list goes on.

Lake Como's crowning glory is its magnificent backdrop of the Italian Alps. The towering fjords rival the grandeur of the Swiss Alps. Other than Switzerland, France and Austria shared borders with Italy to the north.

Several days after we arrived, two of my traveling companions took a ferry to Cerrnobbio. They wanted to see the famous Villa

D'Este. Originally, a private residence, it had become an elegant hotel with a terraced garden and a profusion of fountains.

As they disembarked, several security guards were surrounding the premises. One of the guards told them an event was going to take place there and the hotel would be closed for a week. At that point, my friends believed they had the best inside information about George's secret wedding place.

The next day, with Viviana's suggestion in mind, all of us took the boat tour to the small island of Isola Comacina. After the boat docked, I made my way up the restaurant stairs while looking at the glistening view of the lake.

While walking inside the restaurant, I noticed waiters preparing for a large event. Then I noticed two photographs of George Clooney on the back wall.

In one photo, he had his arm around Brad Pitt. In the other, he stood next to Jennifer Aniston and a man wearing a red, checkered tartan vest.

My mind started clicking. *Were these the preparations for George's wedding? After all, the twelfth of September was just a few days away.*

I turned around and saw a man on the patio wearing the same tartan vest in the photograph. Walking toward me, he asked if I wanted a table for lunch on the patio.

"No, thank you," I replied, "But I would like to know if George Clooney is having his wedding here."

With a teasing smile, he asked, "George who?" He was either sworn to secrecy or he didn't actually know the answer.

A week before we left for home, Mr. Clooney made an announcement. George postponed the wedding for at least another week. He also made it clear that he wouldn't be getting married anywhere on Lake Como.

Gossip spread quickly and tongues wagged furiously about Clooney's newest intentions. Could he be making other plans to keep everyone off track? The same question was posed in Italian newspapers and television programs.

George Clooney and his bride were married in Venice on the twenty-seventh of September. Their intimate gala event took place in the Cipriani Hotel on the Grand Canal.

Brad Pitt was George's best man. Along with sixty guests, the two-day extravaganza included fireworks and a formal wedding ceremony with a five-course dinner. A civil ceremony for out-of-town guests was arranged for the following day.

I wondered why Mr. Clooney had chosen Venice to be married. Perhaps he figured small boats in the narrow canals would limit the number of paparazzi.

Frankly, I think George needs to remember why he chose to live in a fish bowl. Why else would someone be paid millions of dollars to make a movie? Life in a fish bowl doesn't come cheap.

Swinging Seniors in the Single Lane
2014

Being single for twenty years has had its challenges. Just for the record, I've been single longer than I've been married. At this point in life, I'm fully aware that being married is no longer about two people riding off into the sunset and living happily ever after.

When I was growing up on a Connecticut dairy farm in the 50's, I loved watching romantic movies. They always had happy endings. The lovers usually got along and they always cherished each other.

So why did Hollywood make those movies if they weren't true to life? It just wasn't fair to people who were naive, emotional romantics. We weren't ready to abandon the idea of true love. Some of us still hold onto that dream.

When I talked to other senior women like myself, I realized that truth was the same for them. There seemed to be an unspoken law about never giving up.

However, what I definitely realized is that finding Prince Charming is about as realistic as finding Princess Charming. What complicates things is the fact that most single people wear Charming Hats. Those hats were designed to present someone smart, fun, sweet, honest, and vulnerable.

Frankly, it takes a lot of work to hold that pose for very long. So when being human slips out, it depends on how mature people are going to be about letting their hair down under those hats.

Since dancing was my passion, during my travels I looked for places to dance and meet new people. Although women dressed flashier in Las Vegas and the social decorum might vary, underneath it all, people were people. I was told most men and women who attended those dances were really looking for 'the right one.' They just didn't admit it.

I was also told many women my age fantasized about finding a man, but only if they didn't have to take care of him. Many independent single women lost interest in getting married after their kids moved out. Those who experienced the women's liberation movement had a whole new mind-set. It was the end of 'the man is the head of the household' mentality. Now women finally felt equal to men.

It was most apparent when I heard them talk among themselves at dance parties. They were also very selective in trying to decide who the great lovers would be. Unfortunately, the chance of finding such men was on the slim side. Besides, most men still didn't see women as equals in the bedroom.

Aside from swapping stories with friends, they learned about sex in the male-driven porn films and magazines. Unfortunately, sex was rarely discussed in the bedroom, so a woman accepted whatever the man had to offer. It's no wonder he came away feeling pretty satisfied with himself.

Today we have a large group of independent women standing their ground for what they want and they're not afraid to ask for it. Many women were only interested in having fun with a part-time boyfriend. In my opinion, that was also an independent man's dream. He was finally getting the milk for free.

To be sure, there were plenty of single men with that mentality. They were the ones on the dance floor trying to impress women with their dancing, sex appeal, and money. If they didn't have money, they better be charming.

Then there were the lonely people who said they just couldn't sleep without someone next to them. They went through sex partners like a revolving door. These were usually the people on the hot topic list of social gossip. Many were on the dance floor, groping each other and groin-grinding out of beat.

Some of the women were just about falling out of their see-through, skin-tight dresses. Watching a woman in her sixties cavorting around in such a dress was a sight to behold. Those extra few pounds on her undulating hips revealed a dress line rising slowly. That left gawking on-lookers wondering if she was wearing anything at all under that dress.

But she felt so beautiful and sexy. And if she wasn't, he was going to tell her that anyway.

Perhaps she was coy about such compliments by saying, "Oh, no, I'm not."

Or perhaps she gave him the go sign with, "You've got that right, baby."

The final hook was when he bragged about his yacht. He was sure to tell her how beautiful she would look while languishing on his deck.

My job was avoiding those men like the plague. I chose men who danced fairly well to avoid getting my toes crushed. Dancing with men from the New York area was my preference.

As a teenager, I lived in Brooklyn during my last two years of high school. Since most of us knew the same dance style, it was effortless and a lot of fun.

However, New York boys were brash and aggressive. Last week, I met a man from the Bronx who asked me to dance to the famous swing song, *"Rock Around the Clock."* We flowed along the floor like we'd been dancing together for years.

Then he asked me to dance the fox trot. As the slower music started, he pressed his cheek against mine.

"I'm not comfortable dancing intimately with someone I don't know," I told him, pulling away slowly.

He reacted by putting at least a good two feet between us while we danced.

"I didn't mean we should dance quite like that," I said with a smile.

Responding with a wide grin, he said. "But you're such a great dancer, so sexy and sensuous."

I suppose so," I replied. At that point, he looked surprised and thought I was conceited.

"Not really," I said. "That's just what men tell me. Frankly, I would rather they keep it to themselves. I dance like that when I'm alone at home, so I don't dance that way to attract men."

"Well, I'm definitely attracted to you and I thought you were attracted to me," he said.

"I'm attracted to you," I explained. "But not in that way. I'm attracted to the way you dance. You're from New York, so we dance the same and it's easy. But if you think there's going to be more than that, I suggest you dance with other women."

"Wow! You sure put me in my place," he replied. "Frankly, no one has ever said that to me before."

Responding earnestly, I told him about how uncomfortable I was. Finally, he was able to hear me.

While we danced to a slow rumba, he told me most women from Brooklyn were 'loose' when we were growing up.

"I wasn't one of them," I assured him.

My memory was still vivid about kissing marathons with my boyfriend in his car. During those two years, kissing was our limit, even after two hours.

Besides that, I never had a boyfriend when I was living in Connecticut. No one ever asked me out. I didn't go to my prom either. I just lived in my fantasies through those romantic movies and boys I had a crush on in town. I always saw myself as a Plain

Jane. No large beautiful eyes with long dark lashes. No outstanding features at all. I had a tennis player's body, not a womanly shape like Sophia Loren. No wonder no one had ever asked me out.

At my class reunion thirty years later, my life-long belief was dispelled when one of the men admitted to having a crush on me when we were teenagers. He said I was pretty then and was even prettier now.

With cringing apprehension, I asked, "If that's true, then why didn't anyone ask me out?"

"Because everyone knew Jewish girls didn't put out," he responded.

At first, I was shocked. But after thinking about it, I realized he was probably right. In our small class of less than fifty teens, there were only a handful of Jewish girls and all of us were raised to be 'good girls.'

The truth is, I haven't changed much since then. I'm still that old-fashioned girl inside, but I allow my free dancing spirit to surface. I do have boundaries with men and I still have my limits on the dance floor.

Come to think of it, I would never parade around in one of those see-through, skin-tight dresses with nothing on underneath. *Imagine what my mother would think!*

The Snake
2015

Like an ecstatic child, I couldn't wait to see Menaggio again. While renting an Italian villa with friends last summer, I was determined to return this year.

It didn't take long to find a room for rent. After spending two hours inquiring about people who rented rooms in their homes, someone suggested contacting Christina. We met the next day.

After she showed me her condominium and the bedroom for rent, I agreed to rent from Christina. The location was perfect. Her condominium sat above town with a magnificent view overlooking the Menaggio harbor, Lake Como, and the Italian Alps.

Three months before my arrival this year, I sent Christina $2,000 to rent the room for the months of July and August. Since cooking was her passion, I also paid her $10 for each dinner we had together.

Thoughts of making a painting from her balcony excited me. Although I hadn't painted for years, the watercolors were still in my closet. They made their way into my suitcase at the last minute.

Christina's condominium was actually a vacation home owned by her mother. During the summer months, Christina lived there to create more income. Renting a small space in town, she sold her original designs of clothing, jewelry, shoes and handbags. When the season was over, Christina returned to Spain where she lived and made the following summer's creations.

Her family was close-knit. Christina's mother, sister, and cousins lived in Milan. They visited several times during the summer. Eating is a favorite way Italians spend time, so Christina always made her family's favorite dishes during their visits.

Christina's son, Lorenzo, lived downstairs where the basement had been turned into an apartment. He was 21 years old, handsome, lazy and avoided getting a job. Lorenzo spent most of his time having sex with women in the apartment. When he needed money from his mother, they argued out loud until she finally gave in. Lorenzo's grandmother was his other financial support system.

Christina cooked dinner six days a week for at least four people at each meal. Lorenzo and his current sexual partner were usually two of the people at the dinner table. Aside from her passion for cooking, Christina was also an alcoholic who drank wine excessively with dinner every night.

During my stay, some of her friends came for the weekend. Chattering away in Italian, they became happier and louder with each glass of wine. While enjoying their energy during dinner, I also watched the peach and purple sunsets on the lake.

Late one Friday afternoon, Christina and I rode down to the Menaggio pier. She waited there for Sofia, her friend from Milan who was coming for the weekend. When her ferry arrived, Sofia suggested staying for a glass of wine in the outdoor café overlooking the lake.

On our way back to the condo, a man walking in the opposite direction waved to Christina. She stopped the car, rolled down her window and began chatting with Enrique. After he greeted Sofia in the back seat, Enrique was introduced to me by Christina. She told him I was an American renting a room from her.

Enrique was a traveling salesman who lived in the condominium complex next door. He wasn't there often. "I just got back," he said. "I have the new phone models to show you."

When Enrique came to the condo a half hour later, Christina narrowed her selections to three phone models. Then she told Enrique that she would choose one later that day and pay him for it the following day.

As she started talking with him about the view from his balcony, I was surprised when Christina said his balcony would be better for making a painting. Enrique agreed and said he would show it to me after he took a shower.

In my imagination, I was already figuring Enrique was someone who focused on sexual pursuits. The famous line, "How would you like to come up and see my etchings?" came to mind.

An hour later, Enrique returned. He led me to his condo, up the stairs and out onto the balcony. The view of the lake was definitely better for making a painting. However, in the back of my mind, I still imagined it came with another option.

We looked at the view from his balcony for a few minutes. Then Enrique suggested we sit on his settee which had seating for two people. He wasted no time in attempting to seduce me.

After we sat down, Enrique began stroking my hair and told me how beautiful it was. Then, turning to face me, he said, "You are also very pretty."

Pulling away slowly, I sat closer to my end of the settee. As he watched my reaction, Enrique asked if I felt an attraction to him. I told him my only interest was in making a watercolor painting from his balcony.

That's when he started to question my ability to have relationships and said I might have serious problems with men.

"I'm not intimate with men I don't know," I told him.

At that point, he was quick to offer his friendship assuming I would become more comfortable. When that didn't impress me, he finally gave up, accepted my rejection, and started to yawn.

"I'm getting tired and need to get sleep," he finally said.

During our walk back to Christina's condo, I asked Enrique when he wanted to start becoming friends. He said he wasn't available for the next two days and was leaving the following day. I wondered if he finally realized that he had been aggressive with the wrong woman.

The next day, Christina showed me the cell phone she wanted to buy from Enrique. Since she had to leave unexpectedly, she gave me the money to pay him and left quickly.

When Enrique arrived and I opened the door, he was surprised to see me there alone. I told him what had happened and gave him Christina's money for the phone.

Although he neither looked up nor spoke to me, he was able to nod his head as he left. I wondered if he sighed with relief after closing the door behind him.

Christina and Sofia told me they had sex with Enrique a few years ago and that he was a terrible lover. I could have told them that when he looked at me through Christina's car window. They had a good laugh over Enrique, referring to him as an Italian Pig.

In America, women described men like Enrique the same way. After giving it some thought, since pigs seemed so sweet and mellow, I was sure there would be a better creature to identify those men.

Frankly, I think the word 'Snake' really nailed it.

What Might Have Been
2015

When I met Giovanni, he was sitting with Christina at her dining room table. As she introduced us, he looked up at me with a soft smile. His deep, dark eyes were warm and gentle.

Giovanni was also a friend of Christina's family. He lived in Milan and was often invited to stay for the weekend. Christina made dinner for the three of us that night. We ate on the patio and enjoyed a glorious golden sunset over Lake Como. Christina lasted until midnight when the effects of her wine beckoned her to sleep.

After excusing herself, Giovanni and I continued talking until two o'clock in the morning. We shared life philosophies and laughed a lot about ourselves. Giovanni was studying to be a certified yoga teacher while working in the sound department of a Milan film studio.

Drawn to each other like old friends, we were open about our feelings and deep thoughts. Giovanni was a gentle, spiritual man. He seemed to be an old soul at the age of fifty-one. He already knew the best things in life were free.

Later that evening, he told me about his teetering relationship with Serena who lived an hour from Milan. Although they had been seeing each other for a year, Serena wasn't happy. Spending one day a week with Giovanni didn't satisfy her.

After he left Christina's condo on Sunday night, we stayed in touch by phone. I told him my friend Emilio was driving in from the countryside the next day.

When Emilio arrived Monday afternoon, we drove into the mountains where he checked into a hotel. Then he drove further into the mountains where we had an early dinner in a seafood restaurant. Emilio took me around to the side of the restaurant and pointed to an enormous fish tank housing a large variety of fish. Selecting what we wanted for dinner in a remote mountain restaurant was an interesting and delicious surprise.

The following day, Italy was hit with an unusual heat wave. Our plans changed when we listened to the news on Emilio's car radio. A week of severe hot weather would be affecting tourists and locals alike. Homes and hotels on Lake Como had no air-conditioning to offer relief from the 105-degree heat.

Emilio and I barely lasted two days. It was too hot to go anywhere or do anything other than drive around and look at scenery from his air-conditioned car. I was already feeling the effects of my allergy to the intense heat. Both of us were ready to leave Lake Como.

Since he was driving home to the countryside the next morning, Emilio offered to take me to an air-conditioned hotel in Milan. When I called Giovanni to tell him what was happening, he suggested I stay in the hotel which was close to the film studio, and then we could spend time together.

"There's a train station close to the studio," he explained. "I can get to the hotel easily when I am finished working."

When Emilio and I said our goodbyes in the hotel lobby, I felt a twinge of sadness knowing we probably wouldn't see each other again until next year.

"Now it's your turn to come to Las Vegas, Emilio, so I will be looking for you," I said fondly. He smiled in agreement.

Giovanni came to the hotel after his workday ended. Since it was still too hot to walk outside, we had dinner in the hotel dining room. Giovanni headed back to his apartment two hours later, hoping to grab whatever sleep he could get.

After my first night in the hotel, I invited Giovanni to spend the remaining nights. Then he would have a few air-conditioned nights and more energy at work.

When Giovanni came to my hotel the next night, his energy was already depleted from walking to the hotel from the train station in the severe heat. After he came through the door, he stretched out on the bed to cool off. I decided to lie down next to him so it would be easier for us to talk.

He surprised me ten minutes later by turning over suddenly and lifting himself above me. Extending his arms, he placed each palm down along the side of my head.

I heard a ridiculous question in my mind. *Is he going to do pushups over me now?*

As he glanced down, his grin caught my attention. "So you would like me to kiss you, eh?"

In that split second, I was taken off guard. *Would Giovanni kiss me if I said yes?*

Thankfully, the logical side of my brain moved in. *He knows we're attracted to each other, so he's having fun teasing me now.*

"Well," I grinned, "If I wanted you to kiss me, I would have to imagine it in my dreams!"

Although we were together in my queen-sized bed during the next four nights, we either held hands or touched shoulders until we fell asleep. It was innocent and sweet.

By Friday, the heat fell to 85 degrees. Since Giovanni and I were able to walk outside in the late afternoon, we happily spent the weekend walking in his favorite parks and community gardens.

Knowing I had never eaten porcini mushrooms, he also took me to dinner at a restaurant which cooked them exactly the way he liked. They were smooth as silk and quickly became a favorite of mine as well.

During his lunch break on Monday, Giovanni called to tell me Serena had invited us for dinner that night. After accepting her invitation, he came to the hotel and we took the train to meet her.

Serena was waiting in her car outside the train station when we arrived. Giovanni greeted her briefly through the car window while introducing us. After putting me in the seat next to her, Giovanni sat quietly in the back seat while Serena and I enjoyed an easy conversation on the way to her apartment.

It was a hot night when the temperature had risen to ninety degrees. Serena prepared a hot dinner and served it in her even hotter kitchen.

Unfortunately, the air was also thick with their discomfort in being together. Serena told me about her frustration when she couldn't see Giovanni often. My heart went out to her knowing she loved him dearly.

The next day, Serena called Giovanni and broke up with him. Over dinner in a small intimate restaurant, he told me about the situation. We talked about how sad things must be for Serena.

Although Giovanni cared for her, Serena's emotional needs were preventing them from being successful. We talked about Serena changing her mind. She broke up with him once before.

Suddenly, he leaned over the table toward me. As he smiled deeply into my eyes, he asked, "If she doesn't change her mind, you know what that would mean, don't you?"

My first instinct took over. "Yes, that means we could finally play cards!"

I didn't know what else to say. At that moment, it seemed like the best answer for making light of the situation.

The following day, Serena called, begging Giovanni to come back to her. He agreed to try again. It was difficult to hurt her.

Giovanni and I spent Saturday together after returning to Christina's condo. When we sat on the balcony, he began talking about his future. He hoped to return to the United States after

181

enjoying his first trip a few years ago. On his next trip, Giovanni wanted to stay for three months, suggesting we travel together.

Then, changing the subject, he added, "Lately I have been looking online for a house to buy in the mountains. I want enough property for a Yoga retreat, organic gardens, a few goats, some chickens, and maybe a dog."

His thoughts brought me back to my life as a young farm girl. Seeing cows and horses in a pasture still excited me, especially when I could pet them through a fence. I certainly identified with the famous saying, "You can take the girl out of the country, but you can't take the country out of the girl."

"After I buy a house," Giovanni said, "I want you to come for as long as you want to stay." I so appreciated his generous offer.

The next day, we visited Giovanni's sister, Bianca, and her husband, Marco. When we arrived, they were on their front yard patio where tall bushes provided privacy from the street. Since they had no air conditioning, the heat forced them outside.

Hoping the shade and an occasional breeze would bring them relief, Bianca wore an ankle-length, white nightgown with narrow shoulder straps. Marco was in his boxer shorts.

For weeks, Giovanni hoped his sister would be able to meet me. She was fifty-six years old and undergoing cancer treatments. Her prognosis for a healthy future was questionable. Until that day, Bianca hadn't been feeling well enough for company.

Giovanni told me Marco and Bianca loved each other deeply. Hearing those words inspired me to create a video for them. If Bianca passed away, Marco would have a special memory after his grief had passed.

Since their passion was dancing, I asked them to dance together while my camera rolled. Marco held his wife lovingly in his arms as he led her gently around the patio. Dancing in perfect unison, they laughed together sweetly.

When Giovanni told me their children were coming later, I became more excited. Capturing the entire family on video was definitely going to make my day.

Giovanni suggested taking a break before they arrived. He wanted to ride up into the mountains where it was cooler. After he took Marco's motor bike out of the garage, I got on behind him and we headed out. Sitting behind Giovanni gave me the chance to wrap my arms around him as he rode around sharp corners up the mountain road.

When we returned, Bianca was wearing a sun suit and Marco was still in his boxer shorts cooling off with a wet towel around his neck. An hour later, their son and daughter arrived with their spouses. While everyone began having dinner around the patio table, I captured that precious Italian family sharing their delightful Saturday afternoon together.

Although Bianca couldn't speak more than a few words of English, we felt an instant bond. A few days later, I was touched when Giovanni said Bianca called and asked to meet us in a nearby park the next weekend.

That day, while Giovanni and I were resting on a blanket in the park, he saw them coming up the hill toward us. At first, I didn't recognize Marco and Bianca with their clothes on!

Bianca was dressed beautifully in a bright yellow outfit. She wore make-up to enhance her beautiful eyes. On that day, it was hard to believe she was struggling with cancer.

After we all had lunch together, Bianca and I gave each other long hugs as we said goodbye. Then off she went with Marco on the motor bike. While turning the corner, they waved farewell.

Two weeks later, my trip to Italy was over. After I came home, a smile came across my face whenever I thought about Giovanni. My memories were vivid and lovely. I was glad we didn't focus on our romantic attraction. Giovanni was a true gentleman, valuing our friendship as much as I did.

There were times, however, when I did wonder. *What if Giovanni had been available? Would I have been romantic with him then?*

While working my way through that scenario, the first word flashing across my brain was 'fling,' like the one Diane Ladd had in the movie, "*Under the Tuscan Sun*." It was hard to wrap my mind around a fling knowing it came without intimacy and trust.

Over the years, I've realized people are attracted to each other despite themselves. Then the important question becomes, "*What am I going to do about it?*"

If there are no red flags with hidden agendas, the answer would be, "*Go for it*."

Unfortunately, many people aren't ready to see those red flags waving furiously at them. After they closed their eyes, it was too late to hear the answer, "*Move on*."

I remember being like that in my early thirties when I was gullible and naïve. But for me, it was the reverse of, "Don't judge the book by its cover." I believed men were the perfect creatures they presented to me. In my early fifties, I began to see better when I took off my rose-colored glasses.

If Giovanni had been available and we had kissed each other, I imagine uncomfortable feelings would have come up. Since I had thought about it and asked myself that important question, I already knew the answer.

From the day we met, I wanted to be friends with Giovanni with hopes of seeing each other over the years. After he buys a house, if his invitation were still there, I would gladly visit with him during the summer months.

Although my life is wonderful and fulfilling, I do miss being hugged by a man at times. That's why I find dreaming so appealing. There's a lot to be said about dreaming.

After all, I never know when a creative idea will come along and take me along a new path.

My favorite place to dream is in my hammock under my Mulberry tree.

Why?
2016

Whenever I had conversations about religion, it always felt like I was on a mental merry-go-round, dizzy with confusion about what to believe.

The first time I had that feeling was when my mother told me the tooth fairy and Santa Claus were fairytales. At first I felt duped. Then I wondered if she had been lying about big things, like God.

Growing up in a small Connecticut town left me with a limited Jewish education. The only synagogue in town had orthodox services conducted by men speaking in Hebrew. I neither studied Hebrew nor read the bible. My family only attended services twice a year, on the highest holy days. That's when I sat in silence, totally bored, waiting for the hours on end to end.

By the time I was a divorced 28-year old mother, I dared to openly question the existence of God. Looking for help, I arranged a meeting with a rabbi, a reverend, and then a priest. To me, these men were imbued with direct powers from the Almighty. They were surely closer to God than the rest of us, and they were just one step away from perfection.

When I heard their answers, I was dumbstruck. According to each man, there was only ONE God and his God was, without question, THE ONE. Neither man acknowledged the possibility of looking at things any other way. By then, I was more confused than ever about The Truth.

A few years later, someone told me Christians disagreed with other Christians because of their distinct differences. I wondered about that. *If every Christian believed in Jesus, why were their truths different?*

After further research, I found out that some Christians believed in angels while others believed in saints. None of those differences affected me except the belief that I was going straight to hell if I didn't accept Jesus as my savior.

Years later, I was told the Catholic Church had power over its people through guilt and fear. As a seventeen-year old who had a Catholic boyfriend, I could attest to that. I couldn't understand why he confessed on Sunday morning that he had kissed me on Saturday night, knowing he was going to kiss me again during the next week-end.

In those days, I also didn't know various Christian sects were using bibles with different interpretations. Now I was really stumped. How different could bibles be if they were written with directions from God?

This time, I only had one question. *"Why can't all Christians read the same Bible so everyone can be on the same page?"*

I felt alone with my questions and thoughts. Wherever I looked and whoever I turned to, the truth was always different and further from reach.

When freedom of expression surfaced in the early 70's, I was relieved knowing there were other people out there like me. Releasing myself from a conservative life gave me the freedom to explore other ways of thinking and believing.

It was also the era when strict Church doctrines were questioned openly despite the clergy's resistance to change. When certain priests were exposed as pedophiles, that's when hell on earth broke loose.

Cover-ups by the hierarchy made things worse when they fell from grace. People left the church in droves, right along with thousands of priests and nuns.

I met two of them through our travel club. One day, Tom told me about how different their lives were forty-five years ago. When Tom was a priest, Margaret had been a nun.

When I asked Tom why he left the priesthood, he reminded me about that era when other revolutions were surfacing. "The Women's Liberation Movement made its mark followed by protests over the Vietnam War," he explained. "The Catholic Church focused primarily on their prejudice against abortion, birth control, Lesbians and same sex marriages."

Tom and Margaret told me they refused to perpetuate the prejudice, lies and hypocrisy of the Church. It was the last straw. Before they met, each of them walked away from their religious communities in 1970, when they were in their mid-thirties.

None of Tom's reasons for leaving the priesthood included the desire to be married. He was, however, not opposed to it.

"I had looked at the Catholic Church as this especially holy and very spiritual church which was teaching the truth and striving to save mankind. Now I had begun to see how human it was as well as hypocritical in certain ways. For example, many of the priests had fallen in love and were begging to be allowed to marry and continue in the priesthood. This was a firm no-no. So with great sorrow, they left."

He continued by telling me about the Church's hypocrisy. "I realized the Church was betraying me. The powers that be in the Vatican didn't approve of mistresses. But they seemed willing to look away if a priest had a mistress, or was acting out sexually, provided he kept it secret and caused no scandal."

"But to marry a woman, to treat her with dignity, to honor their mutual commitment and make it a sacred relationship, was forbidden. If the Church is all about love, why were they putting priesthood above love? They could ignore lust, but not love. And what did it say about women? Church historians have uncovered some horrendous and disparaging quotes about women from certain popes and other Church leaders through the centuries."

After Tom left the priesthood he decided to marry. He felt strongly, however, about who the woman would be and put restrictions on his search. After meeting several women that year, nothing clicked.

Tom had been raised in a strict Catholic family and attended Catholic schools where Nuns were his teachers. "I had my fill of all that Catholic authoritarianism," he explained. "So I really wasn't interested in former nuns, teachers or nurses. They were just too bossy!"

Although he wasn't desperate, Tom turned to God for help. "Lord, life is pretty lonely. I'd like to meet the right person. How about helping me out here?"

A month later, Tom received an invitation to a wedding. His good friend who lived in Boston was getting married to a former nun. Tom lived in New York at the time and still hadn't met his friend's bride-to-be. However, Tom had an immediate reaction. "The poor man just doesn't know any better," he said to himself.

Since three other New York friends were driving to the wedding, Tom decided to join them. Someone informed Tom that he was going to be sitting next to the bride's close friend who left the convent two weeks earlier.

Tom reasoned with himself quickly. "Okay. I don't want to marry an ex-nun, but I have no objection to talking with one. So I will be nice and join the woman for the evening."

When the banquet started and they met, Tom had an unexpected reaction.

"Wow! She was this beautiful blonde with blue eyes and a very pleasant voice. In the course of our chatting, I asked her what she planned to do now that she had left the convent. She said she

189

was going to continue teaching at Boston College. I was impressed. She was a very intelligent woman. But when she told me she also taught nursing, bingo! Triple bells rang in my head! She represented all three of my disqualifications. Now it was time to run!"

But he didn't. After the banquet ended, fate stepped in.

"I quickly put on my coat and hat and was heading out the door when another friend of the bride asked me why I was leaving. I just muttered something about having to catch the bus back to New York."

When someone else saw him leaving, he stopped Tom and told him about the situation. "People are staying for the weekend and an apartment is being provided for all the out-of-town guests," he explained.

In the meanwhile, Margaret wondered where Tom went. She thought he knew about the weekend arrangements. When she saw him leave, Margaret assumed he wasn't interested in her.

After Tom came back, Margaret graciously agreed to show him around Boston. January temperatures were below freezing and it was windy, but nothing bothered Tom.

"Who noticed the weather? It just felt so good walking down the street holding hands as we wandered through frozen gardens. First we went to the top of the Prudential Tower. Then we went to a movie and had dinner. On Sunday, we attended Mass together. By then, I was hooked!"

Eastern Airlines shuttled Tom back and forth until he proposed to Margaret. They were married six months later in a seaside beach resort in Plymouth, Massachusetts.

Margaret was the ultimate organizer. While making the wedding arrangements, she asked a friend who was a priest to perform the ceremony. After choosing a Pierre Cardin pattern, she made her own wedding dress and completed it the day before the wedding. During the ceremony, Margaret expressed how she felt about her love for Tom. She sang to him while accompanying herself on a guitar.

Forty-five years after gaining their freedom to marry, Tom and Margaret believe they were saved for each other. "We have a great partnership and we help each other grow," said Tom looking at his wife with a loving sparkle in his eyes.

I asked Tom and Margaret if they were comfortable talking about what happened after they left their religious communities. Without hesitating, Tom told me about how his family had reacted.

When Tom left the priesthood, his father was disappointed, but he shed his sorrow privately. Tom's mother was hurt but only talked about it once.

She was confused. "I don't understand how you could be happy three years ago and not be happy now," she told Tom quietly. Then she resigned herself to accepting her son's decision.

Margaret was like a butterfly ready to shed its cocoon. She wanted to step out into the world and do something purposeful with her life While following her training to become a nun, Margaret received her nursing diploma. Then she helped train new nuns while getting both her Bachelor's and Master's Degrees five years later. In 1970, after three years of teaching, Margaret gave up her life as a nun.

She never looked back with guilt or regret. No one criticized or questioned her about leaving. For the first time in her life, Margaret made her own decisions. She wore street clothes and makeup, had her hair done professionally, and got her ears pierced.

After she and Tom were married, Margaret continued working as a nurse. In 1981, they adopted two Korean sisters, ages six and eleven. In that same year, Margaret earned a Doctoral Degree, obtained a fellowship, and became an adult nurse practitioner. Tom referred to her as, "The Iron Lady."

When Tom left the priesthood, he knew he was taking a big chance. Questioning himself, he asked, *"Is this God's will?"*

He looked back to when he was an ordained priest. He had said Mass for ten years before his decision to leave the priesthood. No one made him feel badly about it except the clergy who considered him a rabble rouser. His efforts were thwarted when Tom tried to improve the religious workings of the church.

The clergy officially excused Tom of his duties and reduced him to being a layman. He was never to tell anyone he had ever been a priest.

Tom agonized about being naive during those last three years. He felt like he had gone through puberty and adolescence until he was thirty-eight years old. When his head finally cleared, he was free of guilt and regret. He became true to himself and was relieved knowing he had become a better person. Tom also realized he would have been a better priest who was imperfect, just like everyone else.

He became a youth counselor for a New York state adolescent drug rehabilitation center. After three years, when his ideas for change were ignored by the administration, he decided to leave.

Tom went back to school and received his Master's Degree in school psychology. Two years after his ideas for change had been ignored, Tom left and became a software computer salesman.

It wasn't hard for me to imagine Tom as a priest, but I was glad we met after I gave up seeing priests as super-humans. However, it wasn't easy for me to imagine Tom selling software.

Apparently, Tom didn't see himself doing that either. In 1991, he opened a tutoring center for elementary and high school students in San Diego.

Tom and Margaret now attend Catholic services. They are content in their beliefs while holding firm about the Church doctrines they cannot accept. Tom is finally comfortable in his own skin without the priestly burden of preaching what he was opposed to. As he and Margaret continued their exploration into other realms, they came to believe in reincarnation as well.

During breakfast the next morning, Tom gave me something to read which he had received from a friend. Written by John Churchman, the title was, "Why?" It was the question people asked when they didn't see him in church anymore. John's answer was honest and profoundly insightful.

"Why would I want to be associated with an organization that abuses children and protects the abusers, thus perpetuating the abuse?" Citing other reasons, he asked, "Why would I wish to contribute to the hierarchy that misuses my donated monies intended for the needy by using the funds for pomp, lawyers, and political causes with which I disagree?"

John questioned the church's discrimination against people of different faiths while pointing out their closed culture, lack of free-thinking and discussions about antiquated doctrine. He was disturbed about their claim to be the one true church and then not follow the teachings of Jesus. John concluded that he would always be a true Catholic, but never again a Roman Catholic.

The next day, Tom gave me an article to read about the great number of well-known religious people like Sister Teresa who questioned the existence of God. Sister Teresa startled the world when her diaries revealed the torment she felt from a continual gloom and aching to see or sense God.

I felt comfort knowing some of our most dedicated religious leaders had doubts about God. Although I now had knowledge that affected my life, I still had no answers about death.

Then, unexpectedly, something happened. Inner peace came as I nodded my head in understanding. I knew the answers were neither black nor white. Maybe there were no answers at all. Or perhaps I just had no more need to look for them.

From early childhood and until I was thirty years old, I was afraid of dying. But I was more frightened about what would happen after I died. Today my focus is different. Now I accept whatever lies ahead....or doesn't.

Bottom line, I am still an optimist, hoping God is as we imagine. There are times, however, when I do consider other unexplainable happenings in the universe; so I can accept the possibility of anything being possible.

The way I see it, if God really exists, surely He must be playing a big joke on us. After all, He still hasn't talked face to face with us about where we came from or where we are going.

Maybe He wants us to relax and stop looking so hard. Then we'll have more time to marvel at it all....while we're still here.

Age is a Matter of Mind
2017

During a visit with my friend Fay, she was scheduled to perform with her jazz dance group in their Sun City community center. "We'll be the entertainment during our senior health fair," she explained.

Arriving thirty minutes early, I decided to spend the time wandering around. The array of booths and tables for the health fair were arranged along five long isles of promotional products and services.

The first table called to me with free homemade cookies. Frankly, I was surprised to see chocolate chip treats offered by a dental office since dentists usually tell us to avoid sweets. While smiling at two women sitting behind the table, I said, "I'm actually going to brush right after I eat this cookie."

I was ready to prove it by taking my travel-size toothpaste and toothbrush out of my purse. But I didn't. I just flashed my pearly whites while assuring them I would continue taking good care of my teeth.

A robust man sat at the next table. He asked if I liked milk. Before I could respond, he offered a sample of his natural milk.

I said, "Although milk was a favorite of mine, I don't drink it anymore. It's not healthy for us as adults."

Using my response, he furthered his case, "That's because you were drinking the wrong kind of milk."

Then I told him about my doctor's orders to drink seventy ounces of water a day. "It takes me the entire day to drink that much water, so I don't have room for any other liquids," I explained, while thanking him for his time.

As I moved on to the next table, a woman complimented my hair. Since it had been cut quite short a year ago, it no longer attracted compliments the way it did when my hair looked like a lion's mane. So, at that point, I figured the woman was saying whatever she could just to grab my attention.

She followed her compliment with a question. Asking me to look at her upper lip, she pointed out the difference between the two sides.

"Look here," she said. "Don't you see that there are fewer wrinkles on the left side of my lip?"

Frankly, I didn't see it. I just smiled and said, "Having wrinkles and looking older doesn't bother me." Then I thanked her and excused myself politely. Although I look ten years younger than my age, wrinkles never mattered to me. I just feel fortunate to still be able to dance the night away so easily and without pain.

At the next table, there were services offering help in downsizing and preparing for the intricacies of life in the slower lane.

"Be forewarned," posters claimed. "Don't die and leave unfinished business for loved ones to trek through on your behalf."

It was the first time it felt like I was at a health fair for seniors. While breezing along, there were suddenly powerful reminders of old age and beyond.

There were sales people who were promoting assisted living institutions, services for doing chores when you become immobile, products for incontinent souls and, last but not least, something for everyone: burial plots.

I felt like an invisible hammer had just hit me over the head.
Why haven't I ever thought about those things?
I don't recall being in denial about the inevitable.

196

*Just how long **do** I have left?*

That's when the dance music started playing as the colorfully costumed ladies entered the stage.

When I saw Fay's beaming smile and vivacious energy, it was time once again to focus on the moment instead of the future.

And what a joyous moment it was!

About the Author

Terry Woods wore a variety of hats as an entrepreneur, author, playwright, and magazine publisher.

In 1973, Ms. Woods published her first book, *"Success is at Your Fingertips,"* as a complement to her private-label, beauty product line.

When Terry became a motivational speaker in 1980, she wrote and produced the comedy show, *"A Person for all Seasons."* (Clips of her original show and interviews with an audience in 1987, can be seen on her website: www.seasonexperience.com)

After moving to Ashland, Oregon, she founded and published the monthly news magazine, *"The Ashland Gazette."*

When she sold the publication, Ms. Woods retired and moved to Las Vegas in 1995.

Her third book, *"Climbing Out of the Rabbit Hole,"* was published in 2005. It is available through amazon.com, barnesandnoble.com, and e-books.

CPSIA information can be obtained
at www.ICGtesting.com
Printed in the USA
FSHW021307031218
54199FS